Robert Shufflebotham

Photoshop
Tips, Tricks & Shortcuts

Covers all versions of Adobe Photoshop CC

For Windows and Mac users

In easy steps is an imprint of In Easy Steps Limited
16 Hamilton Terrace · Holly Walk · Leamington Spa
Warwickshire · United Kingdom · CV32 4LY
www.ineasysteps.com

Notice of Liability
Every effort has been made to ensure that this book contains accurate
and current information. However, In Easy Steps Limited and the
author shall not be liable for any loss or damage suffered by readers
as a result of any information contained herein.

Trademarks
Photoshop® is a registered trademark of Adobe Systems Incorporated.
All other trademarks are acknowledged as belonging to their
respective companies.

In Easy Steps Limited supports The Forest Stewardship Council (FSC),
the leading international forest certification organization. All our titles
that are printed on Greenpeace approved FSC certified paper carry the
FSC logo.

MIX
Paper from
responsible sources
FSC® C020837

Printed and bound in the United Kingdom

ISBN 978-1-84078-739-9

Contents

9 Actions and Output 171

Index 189

1 Go Faster

This chapter introduces a set of tips and tricks that you really should be using to work quickly, effectively, and with control and precision, to produce beautiful, crafted, inspiring, Photoshop images and compositions.

Zooming in and out

Don't use this keyboard shortcut if you have the Text Insertion Point flashing in text as there is a danger, when using the Spacebar as part of the shortcut, that you will accidentally introduce unwanted spaces in the text.

Work for a day in Photoshop and you'll find yourself zooming in and out on your images constantly. As with all design tasks, to become faster and to be efficient you should look to identify those tasks that you perform on a regular basis and find the quickest, most efficient and effective way to perform them. Zooming in and out provides one of these opportunities.

Instead of moving your cursor to the Zoom tool, clicking on it to select it, then moving your cursor back into the image to perform the zoom in/zoom out, and then going back to the Tool panel to either re-select the tool you were previously working with or select a different tool – try using the keyboard/mouse shortcut below.

Hot tip

Another good reason for learning this shortcut is that you can use the same technique in Adobe InDesign and Illustrator.

1 Working with any tool other than the Zoom tool, hold down cmd/ctrl and the Spacebar to temporarily access the Zoom tool.

2 Drag diagonally down and to the right to zoom in, or diagonally up and to the left to zoom out.

3 When you release the cmd/ctrl keys and Spacebar you can continue working with the tool that you were previously working with.

Don't forget

If you are working on a Mac, make sure you hold down Spacebar slightly before the cmd key. If you hold down cmd first, the Spotlight Search entry field appears; although the zoom technique still works:

🔍 Spotlight Search

Content-Aware crop

Content-Aware crop is useful when you want to retain as much image detail along the corner edges of an image when you need to rotate and straighten it and/or expand the Photoshop canvas area beyond its initial size. The Content-Aware technology fills areas that would otherwise be lost, to create a seamless result based on existing pixel data in the image.

1 As an optional first step, choose View > Rulers, to show the rulers along the top and left edges of the image window. Position your cursor in the top ruler, then drag in a ruler guide to act as an additional visual reference if required.

2 Select the Crop tool and create the crop. Position your cursor slightly outside the crop bounding box. The Rotate cursor appears ( ). Drag in a circular direction to rotate the crop bounding box. Without the Content-Aware crop checkbox selected, Photoshop automatically resizes the image to accommodate the rotated pixels. Pixels outside the crop bounding box are lost if you accept the crop.

3 When you select the Content-Aware checkbox in the Options bar, the crop rectangle expands to the size of the entire image. Areas of the image along the corners are filled with image detail generated by Photoshop's Content-Aware technology.

Perspective crop

Here's a quick fix for converging verticals – the keystone effect you can get with some images, often most noticeable in images consisting of architectural detail and especially tall buildings.

1 Open the image. Make sure your rulers are showing. Choose View > Rulers to show rulers along the top and left edge of the image window if necessary. Position your cursor in the ruler on the left, then drag in one or more vertical ruler guides so that you can evaluate the image and gauge the degree of convergence that you need to eliminate.

2 Select the Perspective Crop tool from the Crop Tool group. Make sure Show Grid is selected in the Options bar. Proceed to define a perspective crop grid – in this case to straighten the verticals and get rid of the keystone effect currently visible on the building's facade.

3 In this example, click in the top-left corner of the facade inside the top corner of the leftmost column. This sets the first corner of the perspective grid correction.

4 Reposition the mouse (do not press and drag the mouse button) – just move it downward to define what should be a vertical. In this example, down towards the bottom-left of the corner image at the base of the pillar.

5 Click to set the first vertical. Again reposition the mouse – do not press and drag the mouse button – to define the bottom edge. Notice, as you do so, that the perspective grid starts to form.

6 Click to set the third corner of the perspective grid (using the vertical ruler guide as an aid to positioning the click).

7 Again move the cursor to create the final anchor point for the perspective grid. Click. The perspective grid now displays bounding box handles that you can adjust to finalize the perspective crop.

8 Use the center bounding box handles (top, bottom, left and right) to expand or contract the overall size of the perspective grid crop area. Avoid using the corner handles unless absolutely necessary, as you may introduce distortion into the resultant crop.

9 Click the Commit button when you are ready. Reposition the original ruler guides as required to check the accuracy of the correction to the verticals in the image.

Reset Preference Settings

Macs and PCs, Mac and Windows operating systems, and applications like Adobe Photoshop, have come a long way over the last 25 years or so. All aspects of the personal computer technological revolution are now far more reliable than they were in the early days of the desktop computer revolution. But, even so, "things" on a computer can get a bit muddled and mixed up, and start to go awry for any number of reasons. If you experience erratic behavior in Photoshop – on those rare occasions, and they are rare – one of the first troubleshooting steps you can take is to reset the Preferences Settings file. Resetting the Preferences Settings file is sometimes all you need to get Photoshop running smoothly again.

Photoshop loads the Preferences Settings file every time you launch the application. Resetting the Preferences Settings often simply clears some minor corruption to the Preferences file that is causing the slightly erratic behavior. Resetting removes the old file and re-creates a fresh, new file.

If you get persistent technical problems using Photoshop, the cause is probably not Photoshop itself, but some other underlying operating system issue for which you might need to seek professional help to solve.

1 To reset Photoshop Preferences, click the Photoshop icon either in the Taskbar/Start menu (Win) or the Dock/ Applications folder (Mac). Immediately after you do this, hold down ctrl/cmd + Alt/option + Shift keys. Be prepared to hold down the keys as soon as you've clicked to launch the application – it's easy to just miss the opportunity (in which case you'll need to quit Photoshop, then try again).

2 Keep the three keys held down. After a few seconds the Delete Settings File warning appears. Click OK to reset the Photoshop Preferences Settings file.

3 Photoshop continues to launch, and recreates a new Preferences file using default settings. Notice, among other things, that the Start screen no longer displays your

most recent documents, and that all custom tool settings have been returned to their original default settings.
On the other hand, for example, custom colors in the Swatches panel are not lost as these are not saved as part of the Photoshop Settings file.

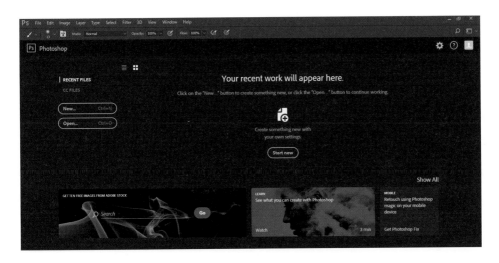

Manually removing the Photoshop Settings file

1 Make sure that Photoshop is not running. From your Mac or Windows Desktop, navigate to the Adobe Photoshop Settings file (Prefs.psp).

Windows location:

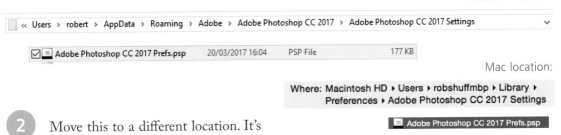

Mac location:

Where: Macintosh HD ▸ Users ▸ robshuffmbp ▸ Library ▸ Preferences ▸ Adobe Photoshop CC 2017 Settings

2 Move this to a different location. It's worth moving it rather than deleting it, so that you have a copy of the Settings file that might be helpful if further detailed troubleshooting is required.

3 Launch Photoshop. On launch, Photoshop generates a fresh default Settings file – at the same location as the Settings file you just removed.

Controlling brushes

Brushes figure prominently whatever kind of work you do in Photoshop – not just when you apply color, but also when making and refining selections and masks, and removing unwanted detail, as well as dodging and burning areas of detail. Master these shortcuts to master your brushes.

Brush size

1 To increase/decrease the size of your brush in increments without having to first access one of the Brush panels, simply press the square bracket keys on your keyboard:

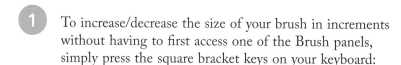

Decrease [ ] Increase

There are some instances where the precise position of the brush or editing tool is more important than the size of the brush. Press the Caps Lock key to convert the cursor to a precise, crosshair cursor. Remember to press Caps Lock again when you no longer need the crosshair cursor.

2 Use the following keyboard and mouse combination to increase/decrease the brush size interactively. This gives you quick visual control over the size of your brush, and it is well worth practicing a few times so that you fully master the technique. Hold down the Alt key (Win), ctrl + Alt/option (Mac). Press and drag left or right using the mouse button:

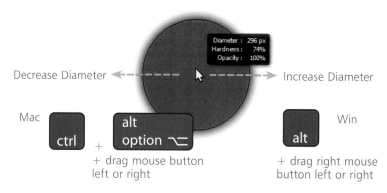

Diameter : 296 px
Hardness : 74%
Opacity : 100%

Decrease Diameter ← - - - - - - - - → Increase Diameter

Mac

ctrl + **alt option ⌥**

+ drag mouse button left or right

Win

alt

+ drag right mouse button left or right

Hardness/softness

Soft edge brushes fade along the edges, creating a semi-transparent effect. Hard edge brushes produce a more clearly defined, opaque edge.

1 To increase/decrease the hardness of a brush using the keyboard, use the following keyboard shortcut:

Decrease   Increase

      +   or   +

These techniques also apply to editing tools such as the Blur, Sharpen and Smudge tools, the Dodge, Burn and Sponge group, and the Eraser tool.

2 You can also use an on-screen mouse/keyboard combination. Hold down the Alt key (Win), ctrl + Alt/option (Mac). Press and drag up or down using the mouse button:

Decrease hardness

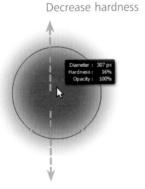

Increase hardness

Mac

+ drag mouse button up or down

Win

+ drag right mouse button up or down

Opacity

Opacity controls how transparent or see-through the color is as you apply it. Use the number keys along the top of the keyboard, not on the Numeric keypad, to change Opacity levels. Values of less than 100% will allow image content on layers below to show through the paint.

1 To change the Opacity, with the Brush tool selected, type 1 to change opacity to 10%, 2 to change to 20%, 0 to change to 100%. Type 47, for example, to change opacity to 47%.

Angle and roundness

To quickly change settings for the angle and roundness of the brush, right-click (Win)/ctrl + click (Mac) to access the on-screen Brush Presets picker panel. Drag the dots on the brush shape thumbnail, in the top-left corner, to change the roundness. Drag the arrow tip in a circular direction to change the angle of the brush.

Pixel Grid

The "Pixel Grid" is a non-printing 1-pixel overlay. This can be really useful if you are working with web graphics where being pixel-perfect is essential, or in other situations where precision is important. Equally, there can be times when the Pixel Grid is visually intrusive and distracting. You need to be able to switch it on and off as circumstances demand.

When the option is switched on, the Pixel Grid appears automatically when magnification goes above 500%, and disappears when magnification goes below that value.

The following example shows how useful the Pixel Grid can be for cropping an image with absolute precision.

If you do a lot of work with web graphics it can be useful to set up a custom keyboard shortcut to switch the Pixel Grid on and off quickly. See pages 28-30 for instructions on how to set up your own keyboard shortcuts.

1 To switch the Pixel Grid off/on, choose View > Show > Pixel Grid. A checkmark next to the option indicates that the option is on; the option is off if there is no checkmark.

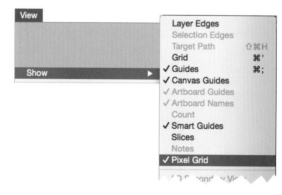

You can use the keyboard shortcut ctrl/ cmd + H to Hide/Show "Extras". Extras are the commands available in the View > Show sub-menu. Pixel Grid is one of these commands, so you can use this keyboard shortcut to hide and show the Pixel Grid. The downside is that this is a global shortcut and hides other elements such as Ruler Guides and Smart Guides that you might want to keep active.

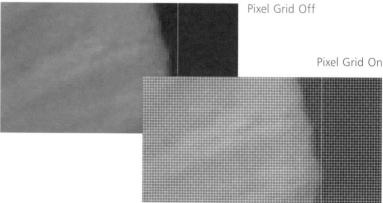

Pixel Grid Off

Pixel Grid On

Recent Files panel

It's amazing how Photoshop projects get complex quickly. And many Photoshop users work on more than one project at a time. When you are working with projects involving large numbers of images and complex series' of graphics, it's surprising how much time you can waste just finding the exact image you want to open.

Seeing thumbnails is probably one of the most effective ways to identify the exact image you want to work with, especially when there are a number of very similar variations of the same file.

The Recent Files command does not have a default keyboard shortcut. It's well worth setting one up. (See pages 28-30 for further information.)

The Photoshop Start workspace gives you the option of viewing thumbnails, but if you choose File > Open Recent, when you are already working in Photoshop, you get a list of filenames that are not necessarily helpful when it comes to selecting exactly the right file. How many times have you opened up an image only to mutter a silent curse under your breath – "No, not that one!" Unfortunately, the Open Recent list doesn't give you the option of seeing thumbnails – which can often make for a much quicker visual recognition, identification and selection.

If you want to identify, recognize and select accurately the first time, use the Recent Files panel.

1. To show the Recent Files panel so that you can identify and open files visually, choose Window > Extensions > Recent Files.

2. Make sure that the Thumbnails View button is selected.

3. Scroll through the Recent Files thumbnails. Click once on a thumbnail to open the file.

Notes

You can position your cursor on a Note icon, then drag it to a new position. You can also position the note outside the canvas area if required.

Some people have 20/20 vision; some have 100% recall. If you're one of those, you probably don't need this tip – skip it and move on. If you are more ordinary and lead a busy life, the Notes panel could save you considerable amounts of scarce production or creative time, and a lot of potential frustration. The idea is simple – the Notes panel can provide an effective, easily managed aide-memoire to some of the complex settings that you might use only occasionally.

You can also use it for handover purposes. If another team member needs to work on the file and follow certain guidelines or instructions, rather than sending a separate email that might get lost or deleted by the time it's needed, use the Notes panel to embed any crucial image-related information in the file – that way, instructions, warnings and guidelines travel with the file and should never get lost.

You can have multiple notes in a document. Click the Previous/Next arrows ( ) in the Notes panel to cycle through the notes. Alternatively, you can click on any Note icon, using any tool, to select that specific note.

1 To create a note, select the Note tool – found in the Eyedropper tool group.

2 Position your cursor on the image. Click to show the Notes panel where you can write your note. An active Note icon appears where you click. Enter the text for the note in the Notes entry box.

3 Click on the Note icon to make the note active and display the content of the note in the Notes panel. The pencil on the Note icon indicates that the note is active. Click on an active note to deactivate it and hide the content of the note in the Notes panel. The Note icon no longer displays the pencil.

You can also right-click (Windows)/ctrl + click (Mac) an active Note icon to access the context menu. Click Delete Note or Delete All Notes as required:

4 To delete the active note from the Notes panel, click the Trash button ( ) at the bottom of the panel.

New Guide – precision placement

The requirement to be pixel-perfect is a significant factor in web and app design. And another significant factor for web/app designers (and for any other designer for that matter) is the need for speed, as development and turnaround times become relentlessly shorter and shorter.

If you are attempting to position a ruler guide manually, at an exact pixel location in your image – you've moved the mouse more than once, and you're now thinking about zooming in to be more accurate – you've already wasted time. Use the New Guide command instead:

Hot tip

Quicker still! The New Guide command doesn't have a default keyboard shortcut. Create your own custom shortcut and save even more time. (See pages 28-30.)

1 You know exactly where you want to position the ruler guide. Choose View > New Guide.

2 In the New Guide dialog box, select either Vertical or Horizontal, then enter the exact pixel measurement in the Position entry field.

19

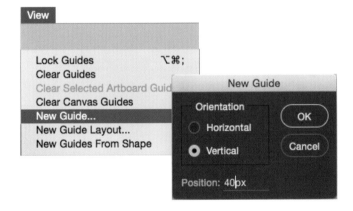

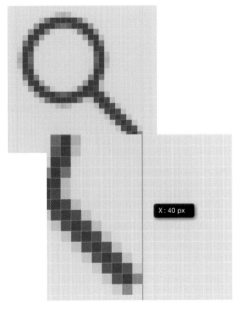

3 Press the Return/Enter key to create the guide, or click the OK button.

New Guide Layout – precision grids

Grids have always been important in design and layout for print, but there have also been abundant opportunities in print to break away from the grid to create interesting visual variation.

On the other hand, from the earliest days, the web has been a more constrained, modular, grid-like design environment – initially with the popularity of frames, then replaced with table layouts and, more recently, "divs". If anything, unlike print, the grid-like structure of web pages has become even more pronounced by the requirements of creating mobile-friendly websites and apps.

If you need to create a strong, clearly defined design grid, the New Guide Layout command can save you a lot of time and effort.

Hot tip

This document is set up as a new Artboard document, with the intention of creating a series of Artboards based on the same layout grid. But, you can also use the New Guide Layout command in a standard Photoshop canvas.

1 Chose View > New Guide Layout to show the New Guide Layout dialog box.

2 Use the Preset pop-up to select from the existing presets, or to save and load your own column presets.

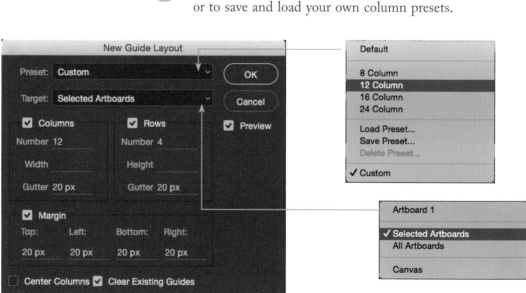

3 If you are working in an Artboards document, use the Target pop-up to create a guide layout for a specific Artboard, or you can apply the same grid to all Artboards.

Creating a custom grid

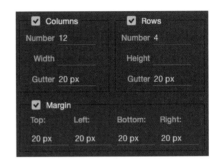

1 Click the Columns checkbox, then create settings for the number of columns you require and the gutter – the space between columns.

2 Create settings for the number of rows you require and the gutter – the space between the rows.

3 Create settings for margins if required.

You don't have to create settings for every entry field. For example, you might just create settings for margins to help define the safe text area for a design.

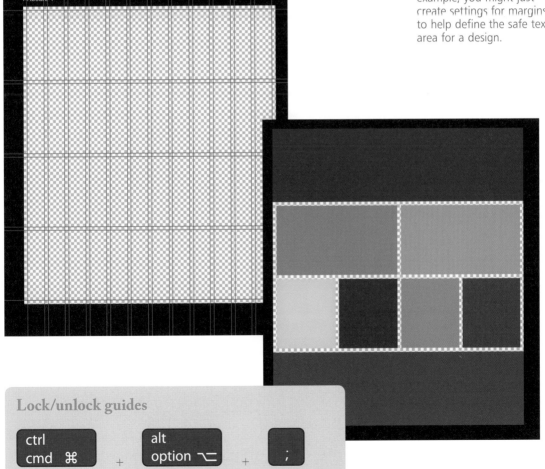

Artboard 1

Lock/unlock guides

ctrl
cmd ⌘ + alt
option ⌥ + ;

Artboard documents

In the New Document dialog box, for Photo, Print, Art & Illustration, and Film & Video document type categories, the Artboards checkbox is not selected by default, but you can switch it on if required.

Artboard documents are a specific type of Photoshop file that enable you to create, manage and refine multiple design variations on individual Artboards, side-by-side within the same Photoshop file. This can be really useful for web and mobile app designers creating mock-up designs that need to be optimized for different devices and screen sizes. They are equally useful for creating multiple versions of a design for an advert or social media post that share primary design elements, but need minor design variations to be targeted for different social media platforms. In essence, each design variation is set up as a separate Artboard in the same Photoshop document, meaning that you do not have to manage multiple, separate Photoshop files.

1 To set up a new Artboard document, choose File > New. From the document type categories, click either Web or Mobile. Notice that for these document types, the Artboards checkbox selects by default.

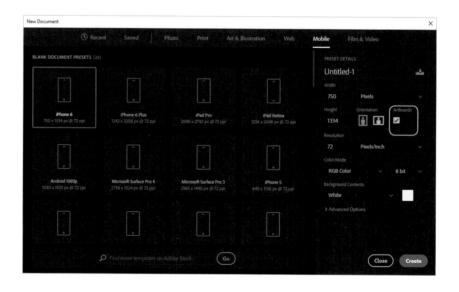

You can convert an existing Photoshop document into an Artboard document. Select one or more layer groups or layers in the document, then right-click (Win)/ctrl + click (Mac) the selection. Choose Artboard From Layers or Artboard From Group.

2 Click on one of the Blank Document Presets to select from a preset list of common device sizes. Artboard sizes are set in pixels. Then, click the Create button. Alternatively, you can enter your own custom settings for Width, Height, Orientation, Resolution etc. in the Settings area. Click the Create button when you are satisfied with your settings.

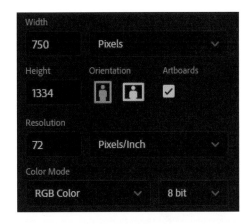

3 Notice in the Layers panel, there is a single "Artboard 1" entry which contains a default layer – "Layer 1". Also, there is no default "Background" layer in an Artboard document.

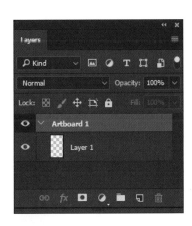

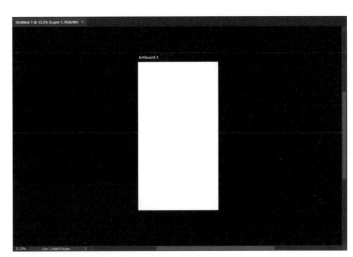

An Artboard document, with extensive canvas area that can contain multiple Artboards of varying sizes.

The Artboard tool

The Artboard tool is grouped with the Move tool. Use the Artboard tool to select, move and resize Artboards.

If you have the Move tool selected, you can click on the edge of an Artboard to select the Artboard tool. The Artboard tool also becomes selected if you drag one of the corners of the Artboard boundary.

When an Artboard is selected with the Artboard tool, Add New Artboard buttons appear along the edges of the Artboard.

When you create additional Artboards, they do not contain a default "Layer 1".

Create and manage Artboards

Working with more than one Artboard makes it easy to set up multiple design variations for a project. You can have multiple Artboards of the same dimensions, or you can have mixed sizes, making it easy to create mock-ups for mobile and desktop devices with different screen sizes. There is a flexible range of techniques you can use to create and manage new Artboards.

Think of an Artboard as a collection of layers that form a distinct page or screen design. Moving between Artboards is similar to moving from page to page in an InDesign document. Artboards can be of the same, or mixed, dimensions.

1 To create a new Artboard, select the Artboard tool. Make sure the Artboard is selected. Click the Add New Artboard button (⊕) on the side of the active Artboard where you want to position the new Artboard. Hold down Alt/option, then click the Add New Artboard button to duplicate the Artboard and all its content layers.

2 A new Artboard with the same dimensions as the current Artboard appears. A new entry for the Artboard appears in the Layers panel.

You can also select the Duplicate Artboard command from the Layers panel menu (☰), or the Layer menu, to create a duplicate of the selected Artboard.

3 You can also create a new Artboard by choosing Layer > New > Artboard. Specify Width and Height settings in the New Artboard dialog box. It's a good idea to give the new Artboard a descriptive name to make it easier to identify.

4 Alternatively, you can create a new Artboard to the same

dimensions as the active Artboard by clicking the Add New Artboard button in the Options bar. Then, click in the canvas area to create the Artboard. You may need to reposition the Artboard if you want it to align exactly with other Artboards (see the following pages for information on using X and Y co-ordinates).

5 To create a new Artboard manually, select the Artboard tool. Position your cursor (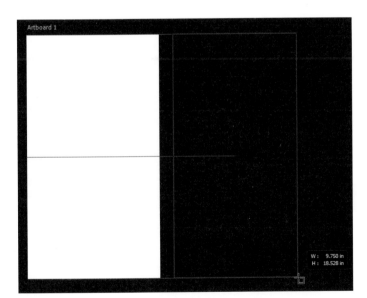) on the canvas. Press and drag the mouse to define the width and height of the new Artboard.

Artboard 1

W: 9.750 in
H: 18.528 in

As you drag manually to define the size of an Artboard, watch for magenta-colored smart guides that help you size and align the new Artboard to existing Artboards.

Controlling the size of an Artboard

As well as using the measurements readout panel and smart guides as you drag to define a new Artboard, you can use a combination of controls in the Options bar and the Properties panel to specify the exact size and position of Artboards.

...**cont'd**

1 Select an Artboard using the Artboard tool. Click the Properties icon in the Panel Dock, or choose Window > Properties to show the Properties panel if it is not showing.

2 Enter values in the "W" and "H" fields to specify the width and height for the Artboard. Enter values in the "X" and "Y" fields to specify the position of the Artboard relative to the zero point.

3 Use the Set Artboard to Preset pop-up in the Properties panel to select from a range of standard preset sizes.

Common preset screen sizes are available in the Size pop-up.

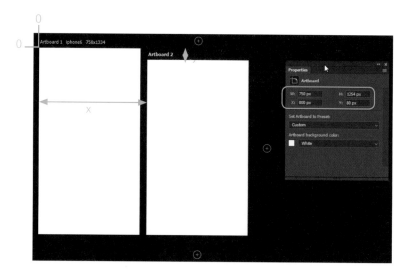

4 You can also use the Size pop-up and/or the Width and Height fields in the Options bar.

Renaming Artboards

When working with several Artboards it is a good idea to give them distinctive names to make them easy to identify.

1 To rename an Artboard, double-click on the Artboard label in the Layers panel. The existing label highlights.

Understanding auto-nesting of Artboard layers

An Artboard acts as a clipping group: if you reposition the content of a layer so that it moves across the Artboard boundary (in this screenshot it's the radial gradient in the background), the content starts to disappear, as the edge of the Artboard defines what is visible/invisible.

The content is not lost; it still exists, and reappears if you drag it back inside the Artboard boundary.

If you drag layer content completely off the Artboard so that it sits outside the Artboard boundary, Photoshop converts this content to an independent, stand-alone layer which appears at the top of the Layers panel.

To move an independent layer back into an Artboard, simply drag it onto the Artboard entry in the Layers panel, or drag it to a precise location in the layer stack of the Artboard as necessary.

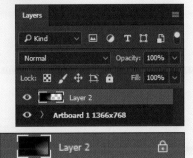

To prevent auto-nesting of content into and out of Artboards – layers moving out of an Artboard and converting to independent layers – you can click the Prevent auto-nesting (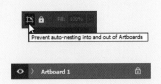) button for the selected layer or Artboard. A Lock icon appears. Click again to release the lock. Note, this does not prevent you from moving content outside the Artboard boundary, but it does prevent Photoshop from creating an independent layer.

2 Enter a custom name, then press the Return/Enter key to accept it.

Deleting Artboards

1 To delete an Artboard and all of the content on the layers it contains, drag the Artboard onto the Trash at the bottom of the Layers panel.

Custom keyboard shortcuts

It goes without saying, to be a fast, efficient, accurate and effective user of Photoshop (probably any software), you need to have a wide range of keyboard shortcuts dancing off your fingertips.

But, it gets frustrating when you frequently use a command for which there is no default shortcut. There are many powerful and useful commands introduced in this book that don't have a default shortcut, which is why it is important to be able to set up your own custom shortcuts.

This sequence shows you how to set up a keyboard shortcut for the Recent Files panel covered earlier in this chapter.

1 Choose Edit > Keyboard Shortcuts to show the Keyboard Shortcuts and Menus dialog box. Make sure the Keyboard Shortcuts tab is selected.

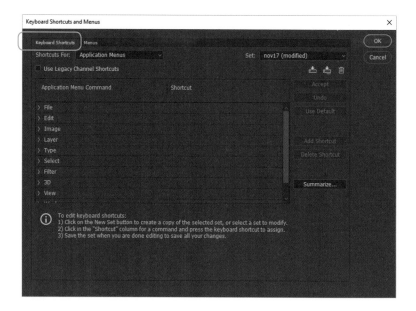

2 To set up your own custom shortcuts you first need to create a new keyboard shortcut set. Click the New Set button ( ). Use the Save As dialog box to save the new keyboard shortcut file. Unless you have a good reason for doing otherwise, it's best to use the same location

...cont'd

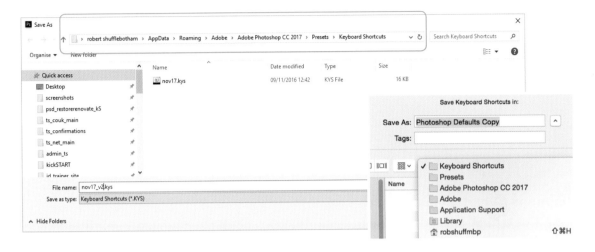

that Photoshop automatically opens: [user] \ AppData \ Roaming \ Adobe \ Adobe Photoshop CC2017 \ Presets \ Keyboard Shortcuts\ (Windows), or [user] \ Library \ Application Support \ Adobe \ Adobe Photoshop CC 2017 \ Presets \ Keyboard Shortcuts (Mac). Enter a name. Make sure you retain the .kys file extension and that the Save as type pop-up remains set to Keyboard Shortcuts (*.KYS). Click Save.

3 In this example, select Application Menus from the Shortcuts For: pop-up menu.

4 In the Application Menus list box, scroll down to Window. Click the Expand button (▶). Scroll down to Extensions>, then click Recent Files to activate the Shortcut entry box.

5 Enter the keyboard shortcut you want to use for the menu command.

6 Click the Accept button if you are going to create more custom keyboard shortcuts.

7 Click the Save All Changes button (📥). Click OK.

...cont'd

8 Check that the command now displays your

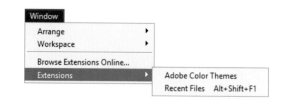

custom keyboard shortcut, and that the shortcut works.

Choosing a custom keyboard shortcut

There are a huge number of keyboard shortcuts already in use by Photoshop and/or the operating system. There are two warning messages you might get if you enter a shortcut that is already taken.

A red circle warning icon appears if you enter a keyboard shortcut that you cannot use because it is already assigned to another command and cannot be changed:

> ✕ Shift+Ctrl+9 cannot be assigned because it is used in Channels panel to target an individual channel.

A yellow triangle warning indicates that if you accept the keyboard shortcut for the targeted command, it will no longer work for the command to which it is currently assigned:

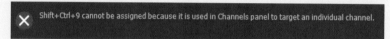

> ⚠ Shift+Ctrl+L is already in use and will be removed from Image > Auto Tone if accepted.

To save you time, here is a range of shortcuts that should be available. But, treat with caution, as even minor upgrades to Photoshop sometimes introduce unexpected and undocumented changes. (Other combinations are available that are not listed.)

Alt + Shift combinations (Win):

Alt + Shift + F1

Alt + Shift + F2

Alt + Shift + F3

Alt + Shift + F5, F6, F7, F8, F9, F10, F11, F12

Alt/opt + ctrl/com combinations:

Win

Alt + ctrl + F9

Alt + ctrl + F10

Alt + ctrl + F11

Alt + ctrl + F12

Mac

alt/option + cmd + .

alt/option + cmd + '

alt/option + cmd + F

alt/option + cmd + Q

alt/option + cmd + P

Alt/opt + Shift + cmd combinations:

Mac

alt/option + Shift + cmd + Z

alt/option + Shift + cmd + .

alt/option + Shift + cmd + ;

alt/option + Shift + cmd + H

alt/option + Shift + cmd + G

alt/option + Shift + cmd + D

Auto-Select

Auto-Select is now on by default: when you have the Move tool selected and you click on an object in a Photoshop file with layers, you automatically select its layer in the Layers panel. This is often convenient and useful – saving you from having to go to the Layers panel, find the layer you want to target, click on it to select it and then bring your cursor back into the artwork to work on the object/layer.

However, there are times in complex layered files that Auto-Select can be less convenient and not what you want to happen all the time – especially as your compositions become more and more complex with masks, varied layer opacity, feathering, and the like.

Use the following techniques to give yourself flexibility, control and precision as you work with layers.

1 Turn off the Auto-Select checkbox in the Options bar.

2 With the Move tool selected, hold down ctrl/cmd. As you move your cursor over the various elements on different, overlapping layers, a magenta bounding box appears around the contents of the layer and "smart" measurement guides appear, depending on where you position your

With the Move tool selected, hold ctrl/cmd and position your cursor just on the edge of the magenta bounding box to display distances to the edge of the canvas.

With the Move tool selected, hold ctrl/cmd and position your cursor over an object on a different layer to see measurements relating to the active layer and the layers your cursor is over.

...cont'd

cursor. For example, indicating the distances from the edges of the layer content to the edges of the canvas, or from the contents of the active layer to the contents of the layer you move your cursor over.

When selecting layers using the context menu, you can hold down Shift and click on additional layers to select multiple layers.

3 Still with the ctrl/cmd key held down, click inside a magenta bounding box to select that layer.

4 Another very flexible way to select a specific layer in complex artwork is to position your Move tool cursor over some of the content on the layer you want to select, then right-click (Win)/ctrl + click (Mac) to access a context menu of layers under the cursor. Click on the layer name you want to work with.

5 The Group/Layer pop-up menu in the Options bar controls whether you select only the specific layer on which you click, or the layer group – if the layer is within a layer group.

Show Transform Controls

Working with the Move tool, if you switch on Show Transform Controls in the Options bar, when you select a layer in the Layers panel the transformation bounding box for the layer contents appears automatically. This can sometimes be very useful, and very annoying on other occasions. Consider switching the option off and using the keyboard shortcut for Free Transform as and when you need it:

2 Selections

Selections are the essential prerequisite to much of the work you do in Photoshop. More of an art than a science, get good at selections, get good at Photoshop.

Selections – adding and subtracting

Hot tip

For detailed explanations of how to use Photoshop's basic selection tools, refer to **Photoshop CC in easy steps**.

Selections are more of an art than a science. You can often start to make a selection with what you initially think is the most appropriate choice of selection tool, only to find that it doesn't quite create the exact selection you want to achieve.

That's why one of the most essential selection techniques in your selections arsenal is the ability to add and/or subtract from an initial selection to make it as near pixel-perfect as you require it or, often, as time allows.

This walk-through starts with a selection of a daisy made with the Magnetic Lasso tool. Overall, it's a good selection, but there are a few areas that need to be removed, and a few areas that need to be added to make it a more precise and accurate selection.

Don't forget

You can use Shift or Alt/ option as modifier keys with any of the selection tools – but you'll probably find that the Lasso tool is one of the most powerful and flexible tools when it comes to fine-tuning a selection.

Adding to a selection

1 To add areas to the selection, select the Lasso tool, then position your cursor inside the existing selection border **1** (in the image on the next page).

Selection tool modifier keys

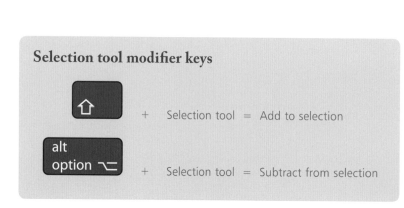

| ⇧ | + | Selection tool | = | Add to selection |
| alt / option ⌥ | + | Selection tool | = | Subtract from selection |

2 Hold down Shift. Notice the cursor displays a "+" (plus) to indicate that you are about to add pixels.

Selections

You can't get far without the need to make a selection – they are fundamental to so much of the work you do in Photoshop.

A selection defines an area of an image that is editable – where you can make changes to the color of pixels. Areas outside the selection are not editable – they are protected from changes you make.

Remember that selections are very temporary – they don't have much permanence unless you save them as an "Alpha Channel" (see pages 38-41).

Selection border – sometimes referred to as the "marching ants".

Editable

Protected

Here's another way to think of a selection (note, this is not how a selection appears in the image window) – it's a temporary "stencil mask" that isolates an area of an image you want to work on, and protects everything else from change.

3 Keeping the Shift key held down, drag across the border **2**, then carefully around the pixels you want to add to the initial selection **3**. Essentially, you are redefining the selection border. Continue dragging the mouse back across the selection border **4** and loop back to roughly where you started from **5**. Release the mouse button. The pixels are added to your selection.

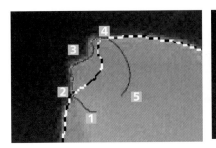

In the screenshot on the left, the direction of travel for the mouse is clockwise, but you can also drag in a counter-clockwise direction. Also note, the mouse trace has been colored red in this illustration, to make it stand out more clearly – in reality it is a dark gray.

...cont'd

The Quick Selection tool is set to Add to selection by default:

You can still use the Alt/option modifier to make it subtract from a selection.

Subtracting pixels from a selection

1 To subtract areas from a selection, select the Lasso tool, then position your cursor outside the existing selection **1**.

2 Hold down Alt/option. Notice the cursor displays a "-" (minus) to indicate that you are about to subtract pixels from the selection.

3 Keeping the Alt/option key held down, start dragging across the selection border **2**, into the existing selection. Drag carefully around the pixels you want to remove from the initial selection **3** to redefine the selection border. Continue dragging the mouse back across the selection border **4** and loop back roughly to the start point **5**.

In the screenshot on the left, the direction of travel for the mouse this time is counter-clockwise, but you can also drag in a clockwise direction. Also note, the mouse trace has been colored red in this illustration, to make it stand out more – in reality it is a dark gray.

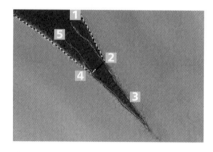

Selection buttons

Add to selection ——
New selection ——
—— Subtract from selection
—— Intersect with selection

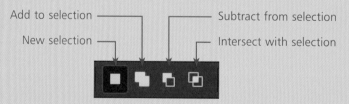

If, for any reason, you don't like holding down a modifier key as you add or subtract from selections, the Marquee and the Lasso tool groups and the Magic Wand tool have selection buttons available in the Options bar. If you do decide to use the buttons, make sure that you reselect the New Selection button after you finish adding/subtracting, so that the selection tool returns to its default behavior for the next time that you use it.

Fill with Foreground/Background color

There are times when you have a selection and you need to fill it with either the Foreground or the Background color. You could choose Edit > Fill to show the Fill dialog box, then make sure that the Contents pop-up is set to either Foreground or Background, then you'd click OK. Or, you could be quicker and more efficient using the shortcuts indicated below.

1 Make a selection. Check that the Foreground or Background color is what you want to use. This example uses the default Foreground/ Background colors of black and white. (See below for the keyboard shortcut to revert Foreground/ Background colors to black and white.)

Fill with Foreground color

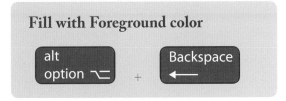

Fill with Background color

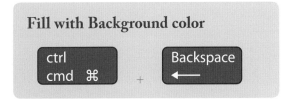

Reset default colors (black & white)

You can use the Eyedropper tool to sample a Foreground color from the image. Hold down Alt/option and click on a color in the image to set a Background color.

Save and load selections

You make a selection using one of the selection tools, then you start to fine-tune it, possibly using the Lasso tool, to work in detail, adding and subtracting pixels; then something totally unrelated that urgently needs attention crops up and you have to deal with it. But, you don't want to have to come back to the selection task and start again from the beginning. Selections, by their very nature, are temporary – for the most part, you create them as you need them; you click away and they are gone. But, there is a way to save selections so that you can reload them at any time. They can be given permanence and saved with the image to be reloaded whenever and however often, as required.

You don't do this for every selection you make – it's usually for complex selections that may take a bit of time to fully form, or for selections that you will need to come back to in the future on different occasions.

When you first open a Photoshop file that you did not create yourself, it's worth checking the Doc Sizes preview (the default setting for the Sizes pop-up readout at the bottom-left of the Photoshop window). When the number on the right of the slash is greater than the number on the left, it may well be that someone has already saved you the work of making a selection. The number on the left indicates the file size of the image when flattened. The number on the right of the slash indicates the file size of the image including additional alpha channels and layers:

Doc: 37.9M/41.2M

Saving selections

1 Make a selection on an image using any of the selection tools.

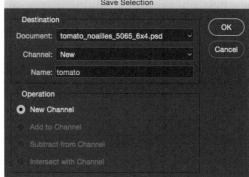

2 To save the selection, choose Selection > Save Selection.

3 In the Save Selection dialog box, enter a name for the selection in the Name field. Notice the Operation is set to New Channel. Click OK.

...cont'd

This results in a new Alpha Channel saved as part of the Photoshop file. It adds slightly to the file size of the image.

Alpha Channels

Don't be put off by the terminology. An "Alpha Channel" is a grayscale channel – consisting of areas of white, black or shades of gray. It's a grayscale mask channel. If you need to, you can paint with Black, White, or shades of gray to edit an Alpha Channel mask.

You can think of an Alpha Channel mask as a more permanent selection – white areas of the mask (when loaded as a selection) represent editable areas of the image; black areas are the mask that protect areas of the image from change.

Click to the right of the channel name to display the channel mask in the image window. (Click to the right of the RGB composite channel to revert to the original color preview of the image.)

Saving a selection creates an Alpha Channel (mask) in the Channels panel. This increases the file size of the image slightly.

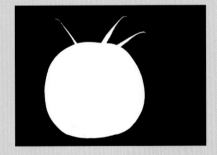

...cont'd

Loading selections

1 Choose
Select
> Load
Selection.
In the
Load
Selection
dialog
box, select
the saved
selection
you want to
load from the Channel pop-up.

2 Click OK. The Alpha Channel is loaded as a selection in the image window.

With the Channels panel visible, you can ctrl/cmd + click an Alpha Channel to load it as a selection in the image window.

40

Saving modified selections

Frequently, you load a selection previously saved as an Alpha Channel, then make some final last-minute changes to it. The active selection in the image window is now different to the Alpha Channel mask. You can easily update the Alpha Channel so that it reflects the changes.

1 After making changes to the selection as loaded from the original Alpha Channel, choose Select > Save Selection.

2 This time, instead of creating a new Alpha Channel, select the previously saved Alpha Channel from the Channel pop-up.

3 In the Operation pane, you can now select Replace Channel. Click OK to update the original Alpha Channel with the changes to the selection.

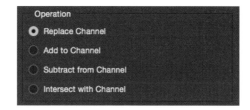

Add, subtract, intersect

There are also channel operations that allow you to use channels to add to a selection, to subtract from a selection, or to create a selection based on intersections. Here's an example of using Subtract to create a new selection using selections previously saved as channels.

Initial selection of sofa, cushions and piping.

1 Start with an initial selection. This can be a loaded selection or any selection you create. In this example, it's a sofa that needs to be recolored. The initial selection includes the cushions and the decorative piping.

Cushions Alpha Channel subtracted from selection.

2 Choose Select > Load Selection. The cushions and piping have previously been saved as Alpha Channels. Select the cushions channel and then select Subtract from Channel. The original selection is modified and no longer includes the cushions.

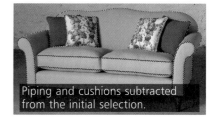
Piping and cushions subtracted from the initial selection.

3 Repeat the process for the piping.

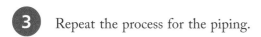

Inverse selection

Here's a simple, clever selection technique that can be a great time saver. Sometimes, especially for complex selections, the quickest and easiest solution is to select what you don't want – then reverse the selection to get what you do want. The technique is a real time saver when you want to make a complex, intricate selection and there is some kind of a background that is reasonably consistent. Sky is often a good example, and also simple background textures, as in the following example.

This is also a good example of where the Magic Wand tool excels.

Sample Size, in the Options bar when the Magic Wand tool is selected

(also available when you select the Eyedropper), in conjunction with the Tolerance setting, also has an influence on the selection. The bigger the Sample Size setting, the more pixels are included in the resultant selection.

1 Select the Magic Wand tool (in the Quick Selection tool group). Check your settings in the Options bar. Tolerance is a key setting – it controls how many colors of similar luminance are selected when you click in the image. There is usually some trial and error with the Magic Wand tool to find an optimal setting for the image you are working on. The default – 32 – is often a good starting point, but be prepared to undo, change the setting and try again.

2 Click on the dark background material to select everything except the blossom.

3 Choose Select > Inverse.

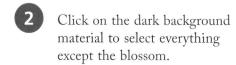

Inverse selection

 + +

Feathering selections

Feathering is a hugely powerful and vital technique in Photoshop work. The concept is easy to grasp – to use it effectively, and productively, can take practice and patience.

Feathering a selection creates a soft transition border either side of the selection edge that helps soften and blur edges so that when a feathered selection is moved or used to create a montage, the selection blends seamlessly into its new surroundings, creating naturalistic and realistic results.

For the Lasso and Marquee selection tools, you can set a feather amount in the Feather field in the Options bar. The downside of this option is that the feather amount remains set for the tool until you change it. If you don't reset it to zero manually after you use it, the feather amount can come back to haunt you if you are not careful. For this reason, it can be more sensible to use the Feather Selection dialog box outlined on this page.

1 To feather a selection using the Feather Selection dialog box, make a selection, then choose Select > Modify > Feather.

> **Feather Selection**
>
> Feather Radius: 3 pixels OK
>
> ☐ Apply effect at canvas bounds Cancel

2 Enter a feather amount in the Feather Radius entry box. Click OK.

The two iris buds in this image are identical – except that one has been flipped.

Feather radius of 2 pixels applied to exactly the same selection creates a more realistic effect, allowing the copied content to blend more naturally into its new background.

Edge too sharply defined – makes it obvious that this bud is not the original composition and doesn't sit naturally in its new surroundings.

Feather dialog box

Feathering using mask properties

Click the Visibility button for the adjustment layer to toggle between "before" and "after" settings to evaluate the amount of feathering required.

Here's a powerful and popular use of feathering to create a vignette effect – where an image gets darker around the edges and corners.

The technique uses layer mask properties – the key controls of density and feathering enable you to create interesting and sophisticated results, all the time working non-destructively on the image, allowing you to experiment and adjust settings until you achieve the desired effect.

Creating a vignette (non-destructive and re-workable)

1 Use the Ellipse selection tool to create an oval selection on the image around the flower.

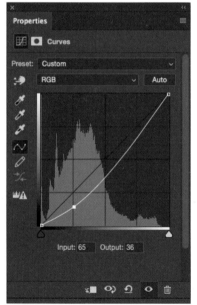

2 With the selection still active, click the Curves Adjustment button in the Adjustments panel to create a new curves adjustment layer. Notice in the Layers panel, this automatically creates a layer mask: this controls exactly where the curves adjustment is applied to the image – white areas of the mask are where changes take place; black areas are protected from change.

3 Edit the RGB contrast curve to darken the image: see screenshot. The result is to darken the pixels within the area defined by the initial oval selection – the opposite of what's required in this example.

4 Now, click the Masks button, just below the Properties tab of the Curves Adjustment panel. This displays the Mask Properties panel, allowing you to control the mask itself.

5 First, click the Invert button at the bottom of the panel to reverse where the curves adjustment affects the image – now the darker areas are on the outside of the image.

...cont'd

6 The next issue to fix is the precise and obvious border between the black and white in the mask – creating an unsubtle and unrealistic effect in the image.

7 Increase the feather amount to create a smoother transition boundary, blurring and softening the transition between black and white – creating a smoother, imperceptible and gradual transition in the image.

More mask for your money

Hold down Shift, then click the layer mask thumbnail to disable the layer mask. This is useful to make before/after judgments on the settings you are using. Shift + click the layer mask thumbnail to reapply the layer mask.

Hold down Alt/option, then click the layer mask thumbnail to hide the RGB composite image and show only the layer mask in the image window. Again, this can be useful for assessing the mask and making adjustments to it if necessary. Alt/option + click again to toggle back to the RGB composite image.

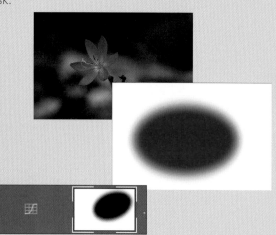

Click the chain button (🔗) between the layer and layer mask thumbnail to unlink the mask – now, you can reposition the mask independently of the image itself.

Paths to selections

There can be times when, because of the nature of the image, it's difficult to make the exact selection you want using the selection tools. But there's another invaluable approach to making very accurate selections that would be otherwise difficult to make. Create a path using the Pen tool, fine-tune the path using the Direct Selection tool if necessary, then convert the path to a selection.

See Chapter 7 – Path Power for further information on using the Pen and Direct Selection tools for creating and manipulating paths.

1 In this example, the difficulty for the selection tools is two-fold: the very smooth curves of the bottle, and the lack of contrast between the object and its background. Create a path using the Pen tool for the object you want to select.

2 Select Save Path from the Paths panel menu in case you want to use the path in the future – always a worthwhile precaution.

3 Make sure the path remains selected in the Paths panel. Click the Load path as a selection button.

4 If you want to add a feather to the selection you create, hold down Alt/option then click the Load path as a selection button, or select Make Selection from the Paths panel menu (▤) to show the Make Selection dialog box. Enter a feather amount, then OK the dialog box.

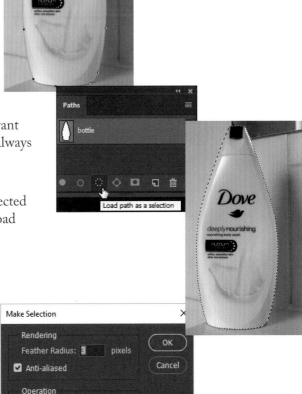

Replace Color command

Make a copy of the Background Layer (ctrl/cmd + J) so that you can quickly look at "before" and "after" versions simply by hiding/ showing layers.

There are times when 100% accuracy is not the primary requirement for the task at hand – speed can sometimes be more important. Here's a command – the Replace Color command – that is frequently overlooked, even by experienced Photoshop users, but it can make quick work of complex selections.

In this example, the requirement is for several color versions of a vintage car for use at 72ppi in an animated GIF intended for use in a Twitter (TM) post.

The Replace Color command works by creating a selection based on similar color values that you can add to and subtract from. And, you can also use the "Fuzziness" slider to control the range of colors that are selected. In some respects, this is very similar to using the Magic Wand tool, but one of the significant differences is that you can continually adjust and fine-tune the selection, which is not so easy to do with the Magic Wand after you've specified the Tolerance value and made the initial selection. Replace Color is good for complex selections that would otherwise be very difficult to make.

1 Choose Image > Adjustments > Replace Color to show the Replace Color dialog box.

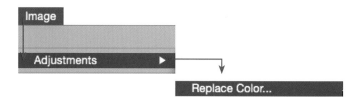

2 The Eyedropper tool is selected by default. In the first instance, click on the blue paintwork of the car in the image window. (You are not restricted to selecting colors in the Preview pane of the Replace Color dialog box.) You can also drag your cursor through an area of the image.

Localized Color Clusters – limiting the effect on the selection as it looks for adjacent or contiguous pixels that fall within the Fuzziness range.

3 By default, the Preview in the Replace Color

dialog box displays a grayscale indication of the selection – white areas indicate selected pixels; black, the unselected areas.

4 You can use the Selection/Image radio buttons to toggle the Preview between the selection mask and the original image.

Edit and refine

1 Use the Add and Remove Eyedropper tools to increase or reduce the range of colors in the selection. Select the Eyedropper you want to use, then click in the main image window, or in the selection mask Preview in the Replace Color dialog box, to edit and refine the selection.

2 Whilst working with the default Eyedropper tool in the Replace Color dialog box, you can hold down Shift so that it functions temporarily as the Add Eyedropper tool, or Alt/option so that it functions as the Remove Eyedropper tool.

Adjust and replace color

1 Use the Hue slider to change colors. Subtle adjustments usually work best. Try to avoid making changes to the Saturation and Lightness controls, as these are important for maintaining the naturalistic highlight and shadow detail in the image.

Recolor with Brush and Blend mode

Recoloring objects is one of the most frequently requested tasks in Photoshop. Here's another technique for quickly recoloring an object with a specific color – particularly useful when you are moving objects between images and you want to recolor some of the elements to complement existing colors in the destination document.

In this example, there are two tulips on a layer. As the requirement is to recolor only one, you can't use a layer Blend mode. Instead, you can use the Brush tool on a selection.

Hot tip

As an alternative, for a more subtle effect, reduce the Opacity of the brush you paint with. Each time you press and drag, you add to the density of the recoloring.

50

1 Set the Foreground Color to the color you want to use to recolor the tulip.

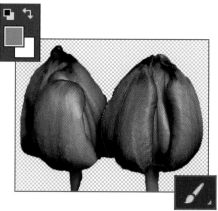

2 Make a selection of the tulip you want to recolor.

3 Select the Brush tool and set a fairly large brush size. Set the Blend mode of the brush to Color. Leave the Opacity set to 100%. Paint with the Brush tool. The selection prevents the new color from spilling out into the other tulip or into the transparent areas of the image.

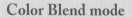

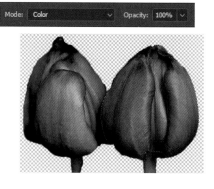

Color Blend mode

Color Blend mode uses the Hue and Saturation components of the color, and does not affect the luminosity of the base colors.

For further explanation of blend modes and how they work, see Chapter 4 – Blend modes.

3 Layers and Masks

Layers and Masks are fundamental to much of the work you do in Photoshop – giving you creative opportunity and the controls you need to work non-destructively on your images.

Isolate layers

Layer masks is one of the most important areas in Photoshop for combining image elements to create subtle, varied and engaging results.

As your artwork becomes more and more inventive, it is surprising how quickly the number of layers can proliferate. Managing, locating and organizing layers becomes an integral part of working efficiently and avoiding frustration and delay.

The Isolate Layers command allows you to temporarily simplify the appearance of layers in the Layers panel by hiding some of the layers.

For example, during a certain phase of working on a project, you may need to check the type settings for a number of different type layers, quickly, easily and without being distracted by a whole host of other layers not relevant to the task at hand.

To select multiple non-consecutive layers, hold down ctrl/cmd as you click individual layers in the Layers panel. To select a consecutive range of layers select a layer, hold down Shift, then click on another layer to select all layers between the first and second clicks.

1 Start by selecting the layers you want focus on in the Layers panel.

2 In the canvas, right-click (Windows), ctrl + click (Mac), to show the context-sensitive menu. Select Isolate Layers.

3 The display of the Layers panel is simplified to show the selected layers only. It is now easier to select the layers you want to activate and focus on – without wading

...cont'd

through lots of other layers. Also, notice the Filter Switch button turns red to indicate it is on, and the filter pop-up changes to Selected.

4 To switch the Layers panel back to displaying a complete set of layers, click below the red dot on the Filter Switch, or drag the red dot down.

5 As an alternative technique, you can multiple-select the target layers, then click the Filter Switch button to activate Selected in the pop up menu at the top of the Layers panel.

6 Or, with multiple layers selected, choose Select > Isolate Layers.

Isolate Layers does not hide the content of layers in the artwork – its purpose is to make it easier to identify layers in the Layers panel by simplifying the appearance of the Layers panel.

Controlling Layer Visibility

Hold down Alt/option, then click on the Visibility button in the Layers panel (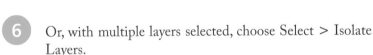) to hide all other layers in your artwork. Do this to simplify complex artwork, so that other layers don't interfere and make it difficult to achieve what you are trying to do. It's usually a temporary state.

For example, as shown on the right, it's much easier to put type around the circle, then create settings and manipulate it, without the visual interference of all the other layers that make up this artwork.

Alt/option and click the Visibility button again to make all layers visible again.

Controlling layer visibility is not the same as isolating layers. When you hide layer visibility, the layer name itself still remains visible in the Layers panel.

Layer shortcuts

The Layers panel is the engine room of Photoshop design. Using even a small number of the following keyboard shortcuts will make you a faster user. The more of these shortcuts you build into your work, the more steam you'll build up – the faster you'll go.

New layer shortcuts

Create new layer:

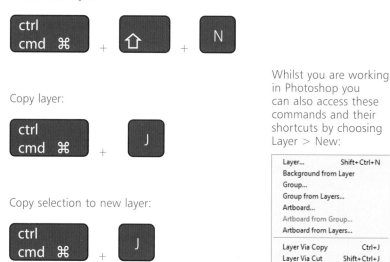

Copy layer:

Whilst you are working in Photoshop you can also access these commands and their shortcuts by choosing Layer > New:

Layer...	Shift+Ctrl+N
Background from Layer	
Group...	
Group from Layers...	
Artboard...	
Artboard from Group...	
Artboard from Layers...	
Layer Via Copy	Ctrl+J
Layer Via Cut	Shift+Ctrl+J

Copy selection to new layer:

Grouping/ungrouping shortcuts

Group selected layers:

Combine related layers into groups to make it easier to manage complex, multi-layered Photoshop files:

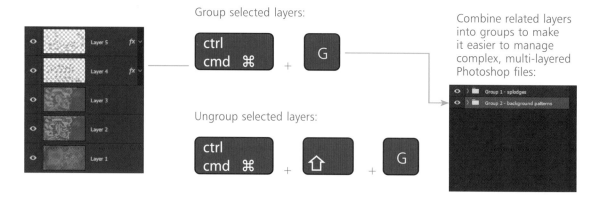

Ungroup selected layers:

Selecting layers

Select layer above active layer:

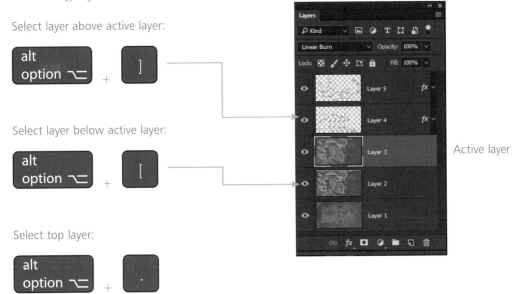

Active layer

Select layer below active layer:

Select top layer:

Select bottom layer:

Select all layers except the background:

Merging layers

Merge visible layers:

Merge selected layers:

...cont'd

Changing stacking order

Move to front/Bring to front of layer stack:

Move to bottom/Send to back of layer stack:

Bring forward/Move up one layer:

Send backward/Move down one layer:

Filling with color

Fill layer with foreground color:

Fill layer with background color:

Essential technique

 +  +

Create new composite layer above the active layer from all visible layers.

This technique can be really useful when you are working on a complex, multi-layered document, such as the Neon type exercise (see page 107-108), and you just need to get an idea of how your current composition and settings would work; for example, if you applied a lighting effect filter.

A quick solution is to use the ctrl/cmd + Shift + Alt/option + E keyboard shortcut.

Remember, the new layer appears above the currently active layer, and is a composite of all visible layers.

You can then, in this example, choose Filter > Render > Lighting Effect. Create the settings you want, and evaluate the results based on the stage you've got to in your artwork.

Retain or delete the composite layer depending on the success of the result.

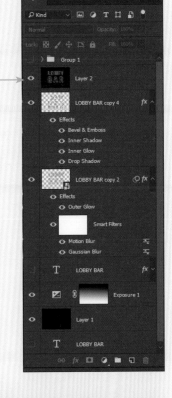

Filter layers

There is a really useful filter pop-up menu in the Layers panel that becomes more and more relevant as your Photoshop artwork becomes ever more sophisticated, involving the use of more and more layers.

Filtering layers is about not wasting time pinpointing and identifying the layer elements you need to work with at any given time.

Kind is the default filter – but no filtering takes place until you select one of the filter options to the right of the pop-up.

1 Working with Kind selected, click one of the layer type buttons to filter the display of layers to show only that one kind. The buttons are toggles – click once to switch on, click again to switch off. You can apply multiple filter types simultaneously. When you click a filter type button, notice the Filtering On/Off switch to the right turns red to indicate an active filter.

The more time you spend working with Photoshop, and the more layers you start to use, the more potential there is to waste time trying to find what you are looking for – unless you master filtering.

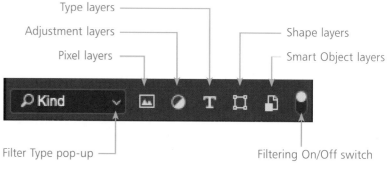

Type layers

Adjustment layers

Pixel layers

Shape layers

Smart Object layers

Filter Type pop-up

Filtering On/Off switch

...cont'd

2 Use the Filter pop-up menu to choose a category that you want to use to filter the display of layers in the Layers panel.

3 Some of the Filter options, such as Filter for Smart Objects, present you with a range of toggle buttons that you can choose from.

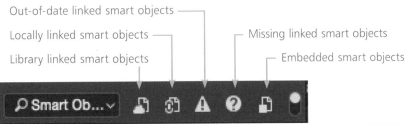

Kind
Name
Effect
✓ Mode
Attribute
Color
Smart Object
Selected
Artboard

Beware

If the Filter pop-up menu is grayed out and you can't access it, it means that you have clicked the Filtering On/Off button (▮) to the off state to temporarily disable the filtering. Click the Filtering On/Off switch again so that it turns red. You can now access the Filter pop-up menu and make changes as required.

Out-of-date linked smart objects ⎯⎯⎯⎯

Locally linked smart objects ⎯⎯⎯

Library linked smart objects ⎯⎯⎯

⎯ Missing linked smart objects

⎯ Embedded smart objects

59

4 Other Filter options, such as Effects and Mode, present a further pop-up menu of options to filter by.

Bevel & Emboss
Stroke
Inner Shadow
Inner Glow
Satin
Overlay
Outer Glow
✓ Drop Shadow

5 The Name filter allows you to enter a search term to filter by.

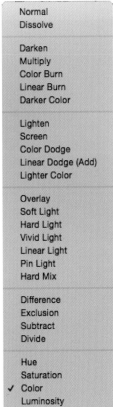

Normal
Dissolve

Darken
Multiply
Color Burn
Linear Burn
Darker Color

Lighten
Screen
Color Dodge
Linear Dodge (Add)
Lighter Color

Overlay
Soft Light
Hard Light
Vivid Light
Linear Light
Pin Light
Hard Mix

Difference
Exclusion
Subtract
Divide

Hue
Saturation
✓ Color
Luminosity

Select and mask – Levels adjustment layer

Select and mask – it's one of the most common and productive combination of techniques available in Photoshop. Together, they allow you to isolate areas of an image so that you can make flexible, re-workable edits and adjustments, with control and precision, to specific areas of an image.

The following walk-through uses a Levels adjustment layer as an example.

The objective in this example is to apply an adjustment layer selectively to specific parts of an image in order to change one area of detail without affecting others.

1 Open your image. Use ctrl/cmd + J to make a copy of the Background layer as a precaution, so that you can revert at any time to the original, if required.

2 Make a selection of the element in the image that you want to adjust and make changes to.

3 Feather the selection edge slightly to create a seamless transition in the image between the areas that you adjust and the areas that remain

untouched. Abrupt changes that appear as seams can make edits appear unrealistic and unconvincing, and may detract from the image rather than improve it. Choose Select > Modify > Feather. Enter a value of 3, then click OK.

Be prepared to experiment with the Feather amount to achieve the required result. Every image is different and you typically find you need a slightly higher value for high-res images.

4 In the Adjustments panel, click the Create New Levels Adjustment button to show the Properties panel for Levels. Because there is an active selection before you create the adjustment layer,

...cont'd

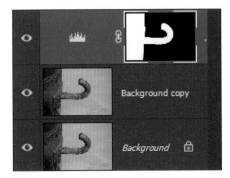

Photoshop automatically creates a layer mask for the adjustment – settings you create apply to the areas of the selection, represented by areas of white on the layer mask thumbnail. Other areas of the image, represented by black on the layer mask thumbnail, are protected from change.

One of the most significant aspects of this technique is that it is non-destructive – you don't actually change the underlying pixels in the image until you decide to flatten or merge layers.

5 Create the settings you require. In this typical example, move the black Shadow slider and the white Highlight slider inward to increase the overall contrast and brightness in the image. Drag the gray Midtone slider to the left to lighten the midtones, and to the right to darken them, if required.

Managing adjustment layers

1 Click the Visibility button ( ) to hide or show the adjustment layer, making it easy to get before/after views of the image to help decision-making.

2 To change settings for the adjustment layer at any time, double-click the layer thumbnail or choose Edit Adjustment from the panel menu ( ).

3 To delete an adjustment layer you no longer require, drag it down onto the Trash, or, with the adjustment layer thumbnail selected, click the Trash.

...cont'd

4 It's sometimes useful to use the Opacity slider to reduce the opacity for the adjustment layer to lessen the overall strength of the adjustment.

Histograms

The Histogram is the visually dominant element in the Levels Properties panel. But what is it and what does it represent? Quite simply, it is a column chart. Each column represents the number of pixels at a particular brightness level (on a scale of 0 to 255) in the image. The spread or distribution of the columns represents the tonal balance of the image. In a high key image, the pixel count is found predominantly in the highlight area (to the right) of the histogram;

in a low key image, in the shadows area (to the left). In the example above, there is a reasonable spread throughout the midtones – but not quite enough shadow and highlight pixels to fully extend into the shadow and highlight areas – resulting in a slightly "flat" image that can benefit from adjustments to the Highlight and Shadow sliders to set the overall tonal range, improving contrast and brightness levels in the image and producing a more pleasing result.

In a "low key" image the pixel count is concentrated in the shadows area.

In a "high key" image the pixel count is concentrated in the highlight area of the histogram.

This example has a reasonable spread of pixels throughout the midtones. A subtle adjustment to the Highlight and Shadow sliders typically produces better overall contrast and brightness levels in the image.

...cont'd

7 mask essentials

1 You can create a layer mask using the Layer Mask commands in the Layers menu. Reveal All means that all pixels on the layer are visible and obscure pixels on layers below; the mask thumbnail starts out white. Hide All means that all pixels on the layer are hidden and all pixels on layers below are visible; the mask thumbnail starts out black.

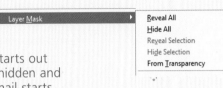

2 Click the Add layer mask button at the bottom of the Layers panel to add a Reveal All layer mask (white thumbnail) to the active layer. Hold down Alt/option, then click the Add layer mask button to add a Hide All layer mask (black thumbnail).

3 Paint with black on the image to hide pixels on the layer mask layer – this allows the pixels on the layers below to be seen.

4 Paint with white on the image to show pixels on the layer mask layer – this hides pixels on underlying layers.

5 Paint with shades of gray on the image to partially hide pixels on the layer mask layer.

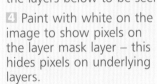

6 Paint with a black-to-white gradient on the image to create a transition that gradually reveals more and more of the underlying pixels across the length of the gradient. (See Mask and montage, on pages 64–67.)

7 To delete the layer mask, but not the layer, drag the layer mask thumbnail to the Trash.

Mask and montage

The more you develop your skills in Photoshop, the more you'll use and appreciate the power of layer masks. Until you either flatten a file, or apply a layer mask, they remain editable and provide one of the most important techniques in Photoshop for working non-destructively on your images.

Layer masks and gradients, in combination, provide the tools to create sophisticated montage compositions where different elements from different images blend together seamlessly to form the final composition.

Assemble content/component images

 Assemble your component images. The images used in this example are all at approximately the same resolution, so there won't be any image surprises when you combine them together.

Combining images with different resolutions

A Photoshop image has a single resolution. If you bring an element from a high-resolution image into a destination image with a low resolution, it appears (relatively) very large, as the incoming element is rendered at the resolution of the destination image.

Conversely, if you take low-resolution content into a high-resolution destination image, it will appear smaller at the destination resolution.

One way to avoid surprises of this sort is to make sure that you are combining images of the same or similar resolutions. Like so many things in Photoshop, this would be the ideal situation – but there will undoubtedly be many instances where you have to use whatever assets are available to you at the time, and transform content as necessary.

2 There are three images used in this example: a castle background image, a medieval helmet and an image with a flag.

3 Create a new document: 6 x 4 inches, at 300ppi.

4 In the castle background image, make a rectangular selection of the castle wall. Copy the selection. Go to the new document and paste the content in. The content appears on a new layer. Transform the contents of the layer to fill the canvas area. (For further information on transforming selections and layers, see Chapter 6.)

5 Open the helmet image. Make a selection of the helmet. Feather it by 1 or 2 pixels. (See page 43 for further information on Feathering.) Copy the selection to the destination document. Paste in; the helmet appears on a new layer above the castle background in the layer stack. Scale and position the helmet as required. (See Chapter 6 – Transform, Reflect, Shadow and Light, for information on transforming selections and layers.)

Add a gradient layer mask

1 Now, add a layer mask to blend the helmet into the background of the castle wall. Either click the Add Layer Mask button

...cont'd

( ) at the bottom of the Layers panel or choose Layer > Layer Mask > Reveal All, to add a layer mask that initially shows (Reveals) all the pixels on the helmet layer – there is no change to the helmet at this point. Notice the layer mask thumbnail is completely white.

Don't forget
The first gradient available in the Gradient Picker uses the current Foreground and Background colors – it may not always be black to white as in the screenshot.

2 It's also important to note that the layer mask thumbnail is active – indicated by the white border around the thumbnail.

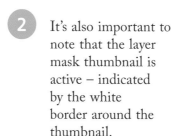

3 Without deselecting the layer mask, select the Gradient tool. In the Gradient picker in the Options bar, select the third gradient – black to white.

Working with gradients

It's essential to understand and master gradients and the Gradient tool in Photoshop. Default gradients use the current Foreground and Background colors. You can select different preset gradients from the Gradient Picker in the Options bar, and you can also create your own custom gradients. (See **Photoshop CC in easy steps** for further information on the basics of using the Gradient tool.)

When you use the Gradient tool, the distance you drag defines the length of the gradient, and the angle at which you drag determines the direction. The gradient forms a gradual transition from one color to another.

Any available space before the start of the gradient fills with the start color, and space at end of gradient fills with the end color.

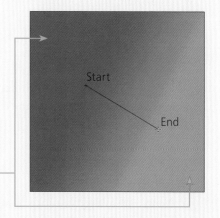

...cont'd

4 In the image window, drag from the bottom-left of the helmet diagonally upward. If you get the result you want first time, excellent. If you don't, drag again to create another gradient – this completely replaces the previous gradient.

Changing layer Opacity settings can also be a very effective way to help blend images together.

5 Notice how the layer mask represents what you've done using the Gradient tool. The distance you drag with the Gradient tool defines the extent of the transition from black to white. Areas of solid black on the layer mask completely hide any pixels on the layer. Areas of solid white completely show pixels. The transition from black to white across the length of the gradient gradually reveals more and more pixels as the transparency changes.

Bring in the flag

1 Make a selection of the flag. Feather it by 2-3 pixels, then bring it into the montage image. Apply a gradient mask and then use the Brush tool, set to a low opacity, to paint with black on some additional areas of the image to selectively hide more parts of the flag.

Toucan tutorial – Layer Masks

Combining images to create the illusion that they intertwine is a fun and quick technique. It can be done using a layer mask based on a selection of the underlying object, and then modifying the layer mask using a brush to partially hide the top object.

1 Open both images. In the porthole image, make a selection of the porthole, then copy the selection to a new layer. Click the Visibility icon (👁) to hide the original Background layer.

 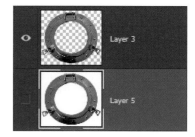

2 In the toucan image, make a selection of the toucan, then copy the selection to the porthole image. Make sure the toucan layer is above the copy of the porthole.

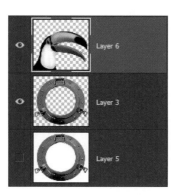 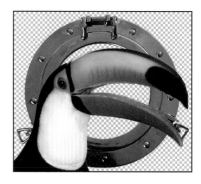

3 Make sure the toucan layer is active. Add a layer mask: either choose Layer > Layer Mask > Reveal All or click the Add Mask button (▣) at the bottom of the Layers panel. A white layer mask thumbnail appears to the right of the toucan layer thumbnail. White means that all the pixels on the toucan layer are visible – therefore, where the toucan and the porthole overlap, the toucan completely obscures the porthole.

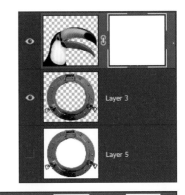

4 Make sure the porthole layer is active. Hold down ctrl/ cmd, then click the layer in the Layers panel to select the pixels on the layer. You now have a selection in the shape of the porthole.

5 Click on the white toucan layer mask thumbnail to make it active. Select the Brush tool, set a hard edge brush, and adjust the size as required. Start to paint on the image with black to hide toucan pixels on the layer mask layer, allowing the porthole pixels to show through and become visible. The active porthole selection makes it easy to limit the mask editing to specific areas of the toucan that you need to remove from view.

The power of masks is the flexibility they offer

So often you need to change your mind, to re-work what you've done to meet new requirements or to give a better finished result. That ability to re-work and re-invent is exactly what layer masks give you – as you edit a layer mask, you are not making destructive changes to any of the pixels in the image. You can always re-work the mask.

In the example below, it is not simply a flip that is required; the positioning of the toucan also needs to be changed. Paint with white, or fill the layer mask thumbnail with white to remove the black areas, then quickly recreate the mask as required.

Vector masks

Don't forget

You can think of a vector mask, in the first instance, as the exact opposite of a gradient mask described in the previous sequence – it is a crisp, precise, mathematically defined shape that defines what is visible and what is not visible.

Vector masks allow you to use crisp, geometrically defined vector shapes and paths to selectively control the visibility of pixels on a layer. But, they also offer considerable flexibility as you can feather the vector paths to blend content in a composition. You can also change the opacity or density of the layer mask to partially reveal underlying content.

This example starts with a document consisting of two layers: a background gradient and an image of tulips.

1 Make sure the tulips layer is active. Create a path or shape. You can create a heart shape, as in this example, by starting with a circle, converting the top and bottom anchor points to corner points, then using the Direct Selection tool to refine the shape (see Chapter 7 – Path Power for further information).

Don't forget

The shape you create initially appears as a work path in the Paths panel. It's worth saving the path you create if you think you might want to reuse it at a later date. (See page 142 for information on saving work paths.)

2 Make sure the tulips layer remains active, and select the path using the Path Selection tool. Choose Layer > Vector Mask > Current Path. The vector mask appears as a thumbnail next to the layer. The vector shape defines which pixels are visible (areas of white on the vector mask) and which pixels are hidden (areas of gray).

Reveal All
Hide All
Current Path

Delete

Enable
Unlink

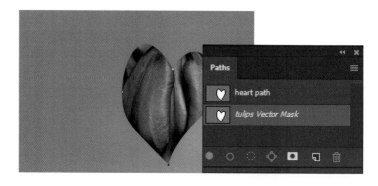

...cont'd

Vector mask properties

The Properties panel offers Density and Feather controls that allow you to create more subtle, varied and interesting effects using the initial vector mask.

1 Make sure the vector mask thumbnail remains selected in the Layers panel (see color panel below). Click the Properties button in the Panel dock, or choose Window > Properties to show the Properties panel.

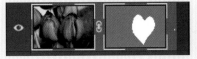

2 Drag the Feather slider, or enter a value in the Feather field to create a feathered transition that softens and blends the vector shape. (See page 43 for information on Feathering.)

(See page 43 for information on Feathering.)

Interface detail

So much of using any software product is about looking for and spotting the interface detail that enables you to work confidently and with understanding. In the case of vector masks, it's important that you can correctly identify whether or not the mask thumbnail is selected or not. Provided the mask thumbnail is selected, you can show the Properties panel Mask settings. If it isn't, do not pass "Go" – the Properties panel won't display the controls you are looking for.

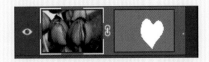

Vector mask thumbnail
not selected

Vector mask thumbnail
selected

...cont'd

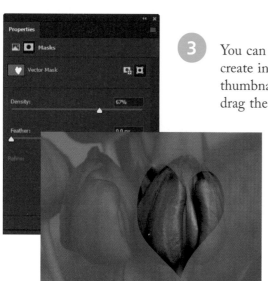

3 You can also control the density of the vector mask to create interesting results. Make sure the vector mask thumbnail remains selected, then, in the Properties panel, drag the Density slider or enter a value in the Density field. The effect is to change the overall opacity of the vector mask across the layer, allowing underlying pixels to become partially visible.

4 Combine Density and Feather amounts to create an even wider range of subtle effects, revealing areas of pixels based on an initial, clearly defined vector shape.

Custom shapes

As well as creating your own shapes to use as vector masks, there's an abundance of opportunities using the Custom Shape tool. Select the Custom Shape tool from the Shape tool group, and make sure that the Type pop-up in the Options bar is set to Path:

(See page 154 for instructions on loading additional shapes to the default shapes set.)

4 Layer Blend Modes

Blend modes – the magic and mystery of Photoshop. Magic because they can lift images from the visually ordinary and unexceptional, to interesting and often stunning. Mystery, because it's sometimes difficult to put into words exactly how they produce the final result.

Layer Blend modes

Blend modes are amongst the most used and least understood aspects of Photoshop functionality. Many innovative and interesting techniques involve a Blend mode to achieve the desired end result.

It is important to understand the basic principles of how Blend modes work – which is straightforward. This understanding will inform your approach to experimenting, and refine the way in which you use them.

It's less important to know a definition of the exact algorithm that the Blend mode implements – you need to know enough to be able to make a reasonably good attempt at choosing the type of Blend mode that you need – then you need to experiment to develop your understanding and control. Don't worry if you can't specifically explain what the Blend mode does – although the intention of this chapter is to help you along that road.

There are some key Blend modes that you will tend to use over and over again – Multiply, Screen, Overlay, Color, and Luminosity – others that you use less often, but sooner or later they all have a use.

Blend modes

The three essential components to blending are the blend layer, the base layer and the result. The Blend mode you apply to a layer determines how the colors on the blend layer and the base layer interact to produce the result. The concept is easy to understand; the results are more complex and, occasionally, difficult to predict.

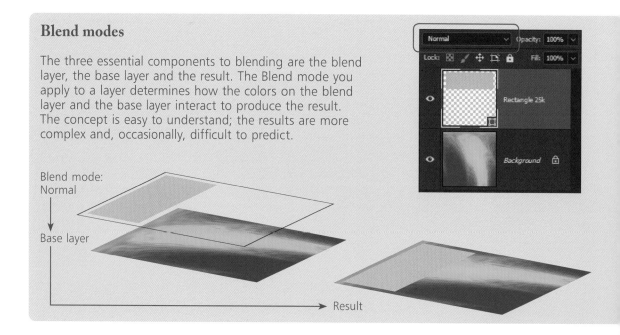

Blend modes are split into six general categories, producing similar effects.

Tendency to darken. Darken, for example, compares the blend and base color and uses the darker of the two. Pixels lighter than the blend color are replaced; darker pixels remain unchanged.

Tendency to lighten. Lighten, for example, compares the blend and base colors and uses the lighter pixels. Pixels darker than the blend color are replaced; lighter pixels remain unchanged.

Tendency to increase contrast. Soft Light, for example, depending on the blend color, lightens or darkens pixels. Lighter areas, below 50% gray, appear to be dodged. Darker areas, above 50% gray, appear burned.

Often referred to as comparative modes – tend to produce extreme results. Divide, for example, examines the color information in each channel and divides the blend color from the base color.

Use combinations of Hue, Saturation and Luminance color components.

Normal is the default mode – no blending takes place (see color panel below). Dissolve simply doesn't fit into any of the other categories.

Multiply is one of the most frequently used from this group.

See an example of Screen Blend mode in use on pages 76-77.

Overlay can be used to enhance slightly overexposed skies – see pages 80-83.

Color is useful for recoloring the contents of a layer – see pages 84-87.

Menu:

Normal

Normal
Dissolve

Darken
Multiply
Color Burn
Linear Burn
Darker Color

Lighten
Screen
Color Dodge
Linear Dodge (Add)
Lighter Color

Overlay
Soft Light
Hard Light
Vivid Light
Linear Light
Pin Light
Hard Mix

Difference
Exclusion
Subtract
Divide

Hue
Saturation
Color
Luminosity

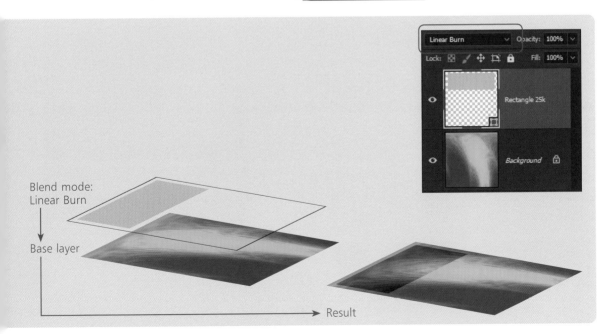

Linear Burn   Opacity: 100%
Lock: ✏ ✛ 🔒   Fill: 100%

Rectangle 25k

Background

Blend mode:
Linear Burn

Base layer

Result

Whiten eyes

Use this quick technique to whiten eyes – one of the most common requirements when retouching portraits. There are any number of techniques you can use to whiten eyes; this one is interesting as it combines the use of selections, layer masks, Blend modes and layer opacity into a fast, efficient method.

1 Make a copy of the Background layer so that you can easily revert to the original image if you are dissatisfied with the result at any time.

See page 43 for further information on feathering selections.

2 Make a selection of the whites of the eyes. Try using the Quick Selection tool; zoom in, and work with a small brush size. Use the Lasso tool, if necessary, to fine-tune the selection. Choose Select > Modify > Feather to feather the selection by 1 or 2 pixels.

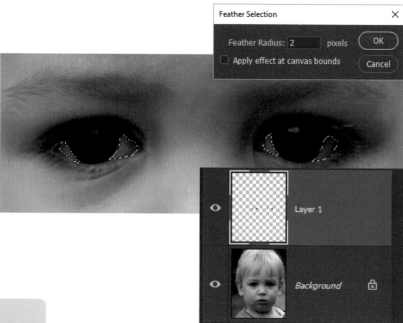

Layer via Copy

ctrl
cmd ⌘   +   J

3 Create a new layer by copying the selection: Layer > New > Layer via Copy.

4 In the Layers panel, select Screen from the Blend mode pop-up. The whites of the eyes become too white.

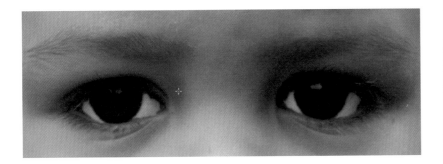

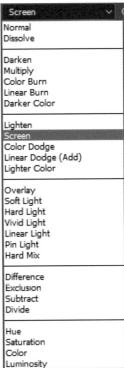

5 Use the Opacity slider in the Layers panel to tone down the whiteness of the eyes to an acceptable level and create a more realistic result.

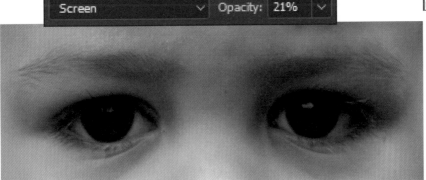

Screen

Use Screen when you want to lighten pixels. Essentially, Screen Blend mode combines the brightness of the blend layer with the brightness of the base layer – the result is to make pixels lighter. Screen has no effect when the blend color is black, and Screening with white results in white.

Whiten teeth

This quick technique to whiten teeth complements the previous technique for whitening eyes – both are frequently used when retouching portraits. Whitening teeth uses a similar range of techniques: making a selection, creating a new layer from the selection, and then a layer mask adjustment layer to produce the whitened teeth.

Remember, the aim is to create whiter teeth, not white teeth: the result should be an improvement – evident without being obvious; naturalistic, not futuristic.

When working with images, color balance refers to the global adjustment of the intensities of the primary colors – red, green, and blue – in an image. The goal is to remove color casts and render colors correctly.

1 Make a copy of the Background layer so that you can easily revert to the original image at any time if you are dissatisfied with the result.

2 Make a selection of the teeth. Try using the Quick Selection tool, or the Magnetic Lasso tool, to select the teeth. Choose Select > Modify > 0. Enter a Feather value of around 2-3 pixels.

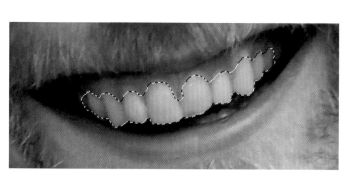

3 With the selection active, choose Layer > New > Layer via Copy (ctrl/ cmd + J). Notice that the selection is deactivated when you copy it to the new layer.

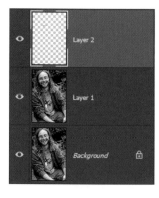

4 Hold down ctrl/cmd and click the new layer thumbnail to select all pixels on the layer. This is important for the next step – because you want to limit the effect of the color balance adjustment layer to the teeth only, you need a layer mask. An adjustment layer based on a layer mask limits the effect to the specific areas you want to affect.

For most general uses of the Color Balance panel, you can usually leave the Tone pop-up set to Midtones unless you have difficult lighting conditions with which to deal.

5 Click the Color Balance button to show the Color Balance Properties panel. From the Tone pop-up, select Highlights to target the changes you make using the color balance sliders to highlights in the image.

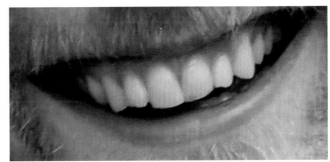

6 In this example, drag the Yellow/Blue slider to the right to add blue and reduce yellow tones. Drag the Cyan/Red slider to the left to add cyan and reduce red.

Color Balance

Color Balance works on the composite RGB channel and allows overall color correction in an image. The Color Balance adjustment works on the principles of complementary colors: Cyan-Red, Magenta-Green, Yellow-Blue. For example, if you drag the Cyan-Red slider towards Red, you reduce the amount of cyan in the image. Drag it towards Cyan and you reduce the amount of red.

Preserve Luminosity – it's usually a good idea to have this checkbox ticked. This option helps maintain the tonal balance in the image and helps prevent the image getting lighter or darker as you make adjustments to color values.

Enhance skies

Sky is a key element in many photographic compositions but can be a difficult component to get right. There can be a tendency, especially with digital cameras, to overexpose the sky, leaving it dull, washed out, and less vibrant than it could be. This is because the camera typically tends to exposes the image based on the main subject you are focusing on.

The aim of this technique is to improve the overall contrast and color saturation in the sky that is slightly washed out and under-exposed.

Photographers use a neutral density filter to avoid this problem and protect the sky from over-exposure. A neutral density filter is darker at the top and graduates to lighter at the bottom, resulting in less light exposing the top of the image than towards the bottom.

This is almost exactly the effect we are recreating in this exercise.

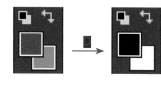

1 Create a new empty layer above the Background layer – either click the Create New Layer button ( ) at the bottom of the Layers panel or select New Layer from the panel menu ( ) (ctrl/cmd + Shift + N).

2 Make sure that black is set as the Foreground color. You can press D on the keyboard to reset foreground and background colors to black and white respectively.

3 In the Tool panel, select the Gradient tool. In the Options bar, click on the Gradient Picker pop-up triangle to the right of the Gradient Picker to show the Gradient Picker panel. Click the second gradient – Foreground to Transparent.

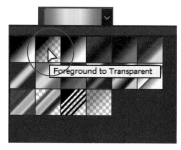

Foreground to Transparent

Get an immediate effect

If all you want is to see the effect immediately, follow Steps 4-7 below. If you want to better learn and understand what you are doing, go to the "Learn and Understand" section on page 82.

4 With the new empty layer active, change the Blend mode for the layer to Overlay. Nothing happens at this stage as there are no pixels on the new layer.

5 With the Gradient tool set to Foreground to Transparent, position your cursor near the top of the image, then drag down to roughly the bottom of the sky in the image.

6 When you release, a black-to-transparent gradient appears on the new layer. The Overlay Blend mode has a darkening effect on the underlying base pixels that fades gradually over the length of the gradient. The effect creates a richer, more vibrant blue sky, and can recover detail in washed-out clouds.

7 If you are not satisfied with the result, use Edit > Undo, and then redo the gradient.
Beware: if you simply drag again across the image layer with the Gradient tool, you combine a new black-to-transparent gradient with the existing gradient – in other words, there is a cumulative effect as you draw each gradient.

Normal
Dissolve
Darken
Multiply
Color Burn
Linear Burn
Darker Color
Lighten
Screen
Color Dodge
Linear Dodge (Add)
Lighter Color
Overlay
Soft Light
Hard Light
Vivid Light
Linear Light
Pin Light
Hard Mix
Difference
Exclusion

Remember, as you drag with the Gradient tool you are setting the length of the gradient transition and its angle. To constrain the angle of the gradient to vertical, hold down Shift as you drag downward.

...cont'd

Make sure you have the Linear gradient option selected in the Options bar:

Don't forget

Learn and understand

If you'd like to get a better understanding of what's happening and the power of Overlay Blend mode – change the sequence on page 81 by doing the following:

4 Use the Gradient tool to draw the gradient from the top of the sky to the bottom – the result is a black-to-transparent gradient on the new layer. This does not create a desirable result, but it clearly shows the initial gradient.

5 In the Layers panel, select Overlay from the Blend mode pop-up to see that it is the Blend mode that is so essential for the success of this technique. (See opposite for an explanation of the Overlay Blend mode.)

Mask out unwanted changes in other areas of the image

Running a black-to-transparent gradient at the top of this image, on a layer set to Overlay, creates a typical problem with this sort of image. The sky is more vibrant with increased contrast and saturation, but it has affected other areas of the image where it is unwanted.

The final stage in this technique is to mask out areas where we don't want the Overlay black-to-transparent gradient to have an effect.

1 Make sure the Overlay black-to-transparent layer is active.

2 Click the Add Layer Mask button at the bottom of the Layers panel ( ), or choose Layer > Layer Mask > Reveal All. This adds a white layer mask thumbnail to the right of the layer thumbnail. (A white layer mask allows all the pixels on the layer to show – in this example all the black-to-transparent overlay pixels – there is no change to the image.) The layer mask is "active" – it has the slightly thicker border.

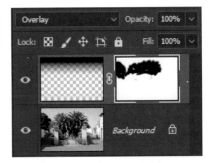

3 Make sure black is set as the Foreground color. Select the Brush tool. Make sure the layer mask thumbnail is active. Paint with black on areas of the image where you want to remove the darkening effect of the black-to-transparent Overlay gradient – you are now editing the layer mask – and notice how the black areas appear on the mask thumbnail. (Painting with black hides pixels on the black-to-transparent gradient so that there is no effect in the black areas. As you paint with black on the image, the layer mask thumbnail updates.)

Overlay

Overlay multiplies or screens the colors, depending on the base color – it is a combination effect of Multiply and Screen Blend modes – it tends to darken areas that are already dark (Multiply) and lighten areas that are already light (Screen). The base color becomes mixed with the blend color to reflect the luminance of the original color.

Recolor eyes

Changing the color of eyes is another common portrait-retouching task. Like any number of edits you undertake in Photoshop, there are times when you want to make subtle, unobtrusive changes that enhance and improve without being too evident and too obvious. Other times, there can be a requirement to exaggerate and take things to the extreme – an exaggerated enhancement to the eyes of a wolf to deliberately suggest an air of menace; brilliant, sparkling white teeth of a vampire for same purpose.

Whichever effect you want to create, flexibility, control and the option to re-work and fine-tune the effect should be foremost in your mind.

1 Make a selection of the eyes – the iris, but not the pupils.

2 Choose Select > Modify > Feather. Enter a value of 1 or 2 to soften the edge of the selection and help ensure a natural blend as you change the color of the eyes.

3 Choose Layer > New > Layer via Copy (ctrl/cmd + J) to create a new layer and copy the feathered eye selection. Note that the selection is no longer active. Hold down ctrl/cmd then click the Layer 1 thumbnail in the Layers panel to select all the pixels on the layer.

4 Select a Foreground color: click on the Set Foreground Color box to access the Color Picker dialog box, or select a color from the Swatches panel.

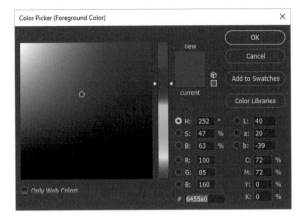
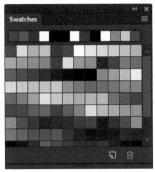

5 Either select the Brush tool and paint over the pixels in the selection or choose Edit > Fill (Shift + F5), select Foreground Color from the Contents pop-up menu, then click OK. Whichever technique you use, the result is the same; it's not attractive, and certainly not subtle, unobtrusive or realistic.

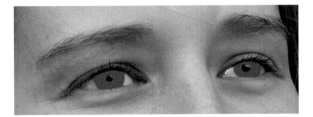

6 In the Blend mode pop-up menu in the Layers panel, set the Blend mode to Color, to apply only the color component of the foreground color and blend it with the brightness of the base layer below, keeping the shadow and highlight detail – the luminance – from the base layer. (See the colored panel on page 87.)

...cont'd

The effect is starting to become more realistic, but is probably still, in most instances, too pronounced.

 Use the Opacity slider in the Layers panel to reduce the strength of the effect by allowing more of the original underlying pixels to show through.

Add a Hue/Saturation adjustment layer for further flexibility

If you realize that the initial eye color you chose is not quite right, you can change the effect by setting up a Hue/Saturation adjustment layer.

 Make sure the copied eyes layer is active. Select all pixels on the layer.

Select all pixels on a layer

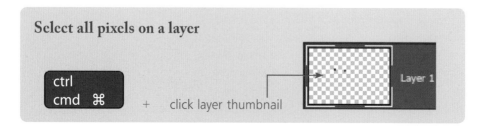

ctrl
cmd ⌘   +   click layer thumbnail   Layer 1

...cont'd

2 Click the Create Hue/Saturation button in the Adjustment Layers panel. This creates an adjustment layer, limited by a layer mask, that affects only the eyes selection on the layer below.

3 Leave the Colors pop-up set to Master. Drag the Hue slider to change the color of the eyes. The adjustment layer mask limits the color change to the original eye selection you started with.

 Black on the Hue/Saturation layer mask thumbnail indicates areas that are protected from change: the change to the Hue only affects the areas that are white – the eyes – all other areas are masked off and protected from change.

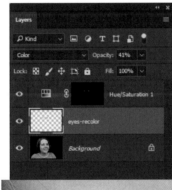

Color Blend mode

Color applies the Hue and Saturation components of the blend color, but retains the brightness or luminosity values of the base layer. This means that in most instances you can change the color of an object, whilst maintaining naturalistic highlight and shadow detail. Color Blend mode works particularly well with monochrome images.

Experiment (quickly) with Blend modes

One of the best ways to get to grips with the effects you can achieve using Blend modes is, quite simply, to experiment. But you don't want to waste too much time going back and forth to the Blend mode pop-up in the Layers panel. Use the shortcut indicated below to cycle through each Blend mode. This is one example where Mac and Windows differ slightly.

Windows

1 Make sure you select the layer you want to blend. In the Layers panel, with the Blend mode pop-up already active you can use the cursor keys to cycle through Blend modes.

Use the Up/Down cursor keys to cycle up or down through the blend modes   ▲   or   ▼

2 Alternatively, you can use the same keyboard shortcut as for the Mac (below).

Mac

1 Select the layer you want to blend.

2 Use the following shortcuts:

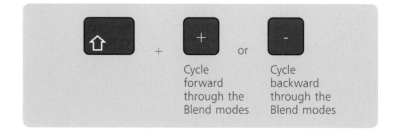

⇧ + + or -

Cycle forward through the Blend modes

Cycle backward through the Blend modes

5 Type

Many images you work on in Photoshop won't involve the addition of type. But as soon as type is required, the skill with which you use and handle it becomes a critical factor in the success, or otherwise, of the finished composition. This chapter helps you achieve speed and accuracy in the way you style your type, as well as demonstrating some creative uses and effects.

Type Size shortcuts

Practice these shortcuts a few times so that they become automatic – it will be time well spent.

There are some keyboard shortcuts that you should not be prepared to live without – the shortcuts for scaling type are notable amongst those: not least because if you learn them for Photoshop, you can transfer exactly the same techniques to Adobe InDesign and Illustrator.

1 To quickly scale type using keyboard shortcuts, first select the type, then use the keyboard shortcut combinations indicated below.

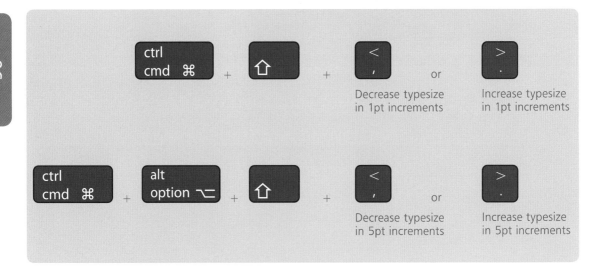

In the Layers panel, double-click the Type layer thumbnail to quickly select the text on the layer.

Scale type visually

Here's another essential tip for scaling type – it allows you to work visually, quickly and interactively, on-screen, using your mouse and keyboard. In this example, the aim is to quickly scale the heading so that it matches the width of the margin guides set for this Artboard.

Switch on the Show Transform Controls checkbox (see page 32) before you select the Type layer, to display the eight transformation handles around the perimeter of the type object.

1 Select the type layer you want to work on. Make sure that the Show Transform Controls checkbox is selected in the Options bar. The type object displays a bounding box with eight transformation handles around the perimeter.

2 Hold down Shift. Position your cursor on any of the corner handles. Drag diagonally to resize the type in proportion.

3 Release the mouse button, then the Shift key, when the type is the desired size.

Tracking and Kerning

Tracking increases or decreases the space between characters across a range of selected text; Kerning increases or decreases (but is most often used to decrease) the space between pairs of characters.

Tracking and Kerning provide the possibility of interesting variation and attractive typesetting that can help the viewer become visually involved with the artwork in front of them. The keyboard shortcuts for Tracking and Kerning are identical.

1 For Kerning, click to place the text insertion point between the pair of characters you want to kern; for Tracking, highlight the range of text you want to track before you use the controls in the Character panel or the keyboard shortcuts indicated below.

2 Click the Character and Paragraph panel button in the Options bar, when you have text selected, to reveal the Character panel where you can see a numeric readout of the Tracking/ Kerning values as you use the keyboard shortcut.

the LOST & HUNGRY TRAVELLER

the LOST & HUNGRY TRAVELLER

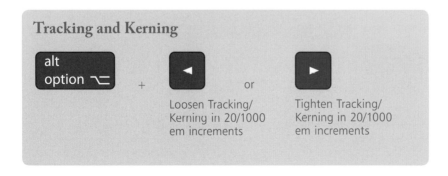

Tracking and Kerning

alt option ⌥ + ◄ or ►

Loosen Tracking/ Kerning in 20/1000 em increments

Tighten Tracking/ Kerning in 20/1000 em increments

Baseline Shift

All type sits on an imaginary line called the baseline. As in Adobe InDesign and Illustrator, Photoshop offers controls to baseline shift selected characters above or below their baseline. This can be essential when working with type on a path in order to position the type exactly where it needs to be to create a crafted, precise result. Baseline Shift can also be useful for adding visual interest and playfulness to words in a piece of artwork.

Be really careful after you use Baseline Shift on text – settings remain in force and can come back to haunt you. Baseline Shift is a special effect and is not required for normal text. Reset the Baseline Shift field to zero when you've finished using it.

1 Working with the Type tool, select an individual character or a range of text characters that you want to baseline shift.

2 Click the Character and Paragraph panel button in the Options bar to show the Character panel, where you can see a readout of the baseline shift value when you use the keyboard shortcut at the bottom of this page.

Tracking and Baseline Shift controls are essential to achieve polished, finely-worked results.

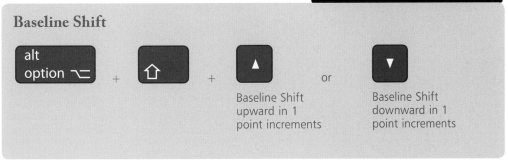

Baseline Shift

alt / option ⌥ + ⇧ + ▲   or   ▼

Baseline Shift upward in 1 point increments

Baseline Shift downward in 1 point increments

Leading

The use of Leading is one of the critical factors when judging the success of type in a project.

Too little Leading, and the type becomes awkward and difficult to read; it is too dense on the page and becomes off-putting. Too much Leading, and the type and the meaning it conveys can become disjointed and lacking cohesion, and the impact and meaning of the written content itself is lost or reduced.

Get it right, and it creates a pleasing, balanced and attractive reading environment, enhancing the content and inviting the viewer in to read. The importance of choosing a suitable Leading value in conjunction with an appropriate type size cannot be overstated.

Using keyboard shortcuts for Leading means that you have the ability at your fingertips to quickly create, fine-tune and edit settings quickly, easily and interactively.

Leading is the distance from one baseline of type to another:

The quick lazy lumping lolloping brown fox flew the fences with ease

Leading

Leading values you set become the default setting for the next type object you create – take care and always double-check your Character panel so that unintentional settings don't come back to haunt you.

Leading is a Character setting. Make sure you highlight the range of text where you want to change the Leading, or select the entire text object to change all text in that object.

Leading

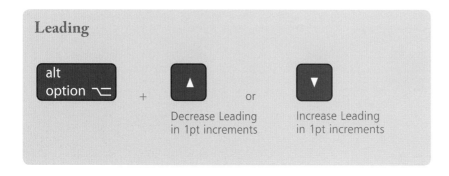

alt
option ⌥

+

▲
Decrease Leading in 1pt increments

or

▼
Increase Leading in 1pt increments

2 Use the keyboard shortcuts indicated below to adjust Leading in 1-point increments.

3 To get a readout for the Leading value of selected text, click the Character/Paragraph panel button ( ) in the Options bar to show the Character and Paragraph panels.

The default value for Auto Leading is 120% of the point size with which you are working.

At the edge of the day, at the edge of the sea, close to exhaustion, the hungry traveller pauses and contemplates distances travelled, distances and seasons to come.

At the edge of the day, at the edge of the sea, close to exhaustion, the hungry traveller pauses and contemplates distances travelled, distances and seasons to come.

At the edge of the day, at the edge of the sea, close to exhaustion, the hungry traveller pauses and contemplates distances travelled, distances and seasons to come.

Auto Leading: 16/ Auto   16 /22pt   16/16pt

Auto Leading v Absolute/Fixed Leading

Auto Leading sets the Leading value to 120% of the type size. For example, if you have 10 point type, the Auto Leading value is 12 points. The benefit of Auto Leading is that you get reasonably good, acceptable results across a wide range of type sizes and, if you change your type size, the Leading value changes automatically to retain the same 120% of type size.

If you set an absolute or fixed value, you can achieve more precise, more sophisticated typesetting results, but, if you change your type size, you must then make a decision about changing the Leading value to keep the balance and proportions of type size to Leading.

If you have set an absolute value for Leading and you want to revert to Auto Leading, choose Auto from the Leading pop-up in the Character panel.

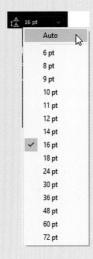

Paragraph Styles

One of the most overlooked features for handling type in Photoshop is, surprisingly, the provision of paragraph and character styles. Use paragraph and character styles to apply type styling quickly, efficiently and accurately to maintain and ensure consistency in a related series of documents; for example, to implement a corporate brand identity consistently.

1 Copy text from a word-processed document.

2 In Photoshop, create a text area using the Horizontal Type tool. Choose Edit > Paste to paste the text into the text area. Alternatively, type text directly into the area type frame.

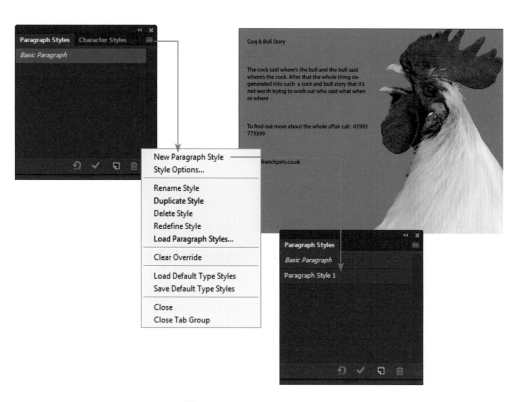

3 Choose Window > Paragraph Styles to show the Paragraph Styles panel (initially grouped with the Character Styles panel).

4 Make sure the type layer is active, and that the Text Insertion Point is flashing in a paragraph.

5 Go to the Paragraph Styles panel menu (■) and select New Paragraph Style.

6 "Paragraph Style 1" appears in the Paragraph Styles panel. Click on the Paragraph Style 1 entry, if necessary, to select it.

Provided the Text Insertion Point is active in a paragraph of text, click the Preview checkbox to see changes applied to text as you change settings.

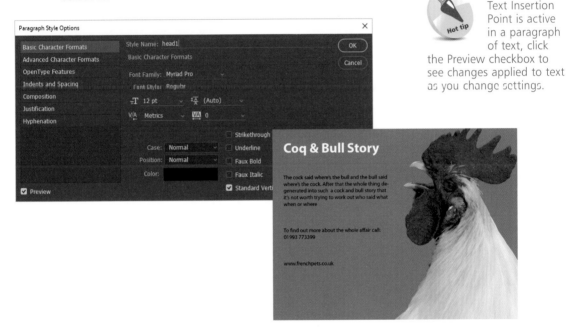

7 Go to the panel menu (■) and select Style Options to show the Paragraph Style Options dialog box.

8 Enter a name in the Style Name entry field. Click on each typesetting category on the left of the dialog box in turn, and create type settings as required. Click OK.

9 To apply a paragraph style, either click to place the Text Insertion Point in a single paragraph, or drag across a range of paragraphs to select multiple paragraphs. Click on the paragraph style in the Paragraph Styles panel.

...cont'd

If you see "+" next to the Paragraph Style, you may need to click the Clear Override button at the bottom of the panel to remove any manual formatting (overrides) already applied to the type:

If you have a Text layer active and you click on a Paragraph Style, you apply the Paragraph Style to the entire layer.

Try this Quick Technique

This is a any easy way to create a Paragraph Style based on type settings already applied to some existing text.

1 Highlight a paragraph of text and create the type settings you want to use. When you are satisfied with the results, make sure you keep the type selected – these settings now form a model for a Paragraph Style.

2 Select New Paragraph Style from the Paragraph Styles panel menu (▤). The settings from the selected text are automatically set in the Paragraph Style Options dialog box.

3 You can double-click the default Paragraph Style name to show the Paragraph Style Options dialog box to enter a name for the style.

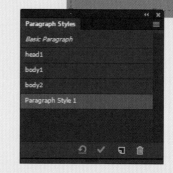

Redefine Styles

There are occasions when you manually change settings on a paragraph that has a paragraph style applied. Then you realize that this is what the paragraph style should look like. You can redefine the style – based on these new settings.

1 Highlight a paragraph of text that already has a paragraph style applied to it. Make some manual formatting changes to the type (in this example, change the title color to cyan). These are the formatting changes that you now want to become permanent inclusions in the style.

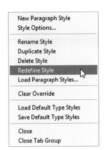

2 With the type with changed settings still selected, go to the Paragraph Styles panel menu (▤). Select Redefine Style. The Paragraph Style updates with the new settings, as do any paragraphs where the style is already applied.

Character Styles

Use Paragraph Styles to set type formatting for an entire paragraph or for a range of selected paragraphs. Use Character Styles to ensure consistency, speed and accuracy when you want to apply type formatting at a sub-paragraph level – anything from a single character to a word or phrase, but typically not the entire paragraph.

1 Click on a layer other than a type layer. From the Character Styles panel menu (▤) select New Character Style. "Character Style 1" appears in the Character Styles panel.

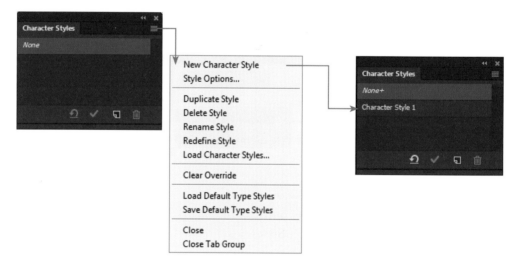

2 Double-click Character Style 1 to show the Character Style Options dialog box.

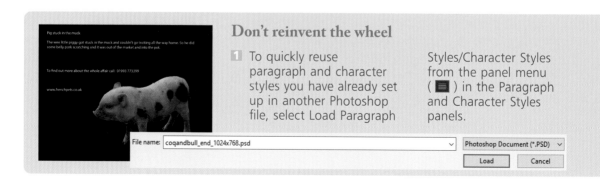

Don't reinvent the wheel

1 To quickly reuse paragraph and character styles you have already set up in another Photoshop file, select Load Paragraph Styles/Character Styles from the panel menu (▤) in the Paragraph and Character Styles panels.

...cont'd

3 Click on each of the categories on the left-hand side of the dialog box and create the set of character attributes you want to apply as a character style. Click OK.

If you have a text layer selected when you create or edit settings for a character style, the settings apply to all the text on that layer.

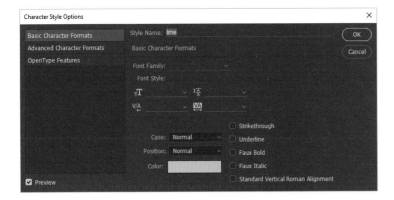

4 To apply a character style, highlight a character, word or phrase, then click on the name of the character style in the Character Styles panel.

2 Use standard Mac/ Windows techniques to navigate to the Photoshop document with the styles you want to copy.

3 Click the Load button to copy the styles to the Paragraph/Character Styles panel in the active document.

Get your Glyphs out

A glyph is a unique, individual instance of a letterform. For example, the screenshot below shows the alternate glyphs for lowercase "y" in Warnock Pro Regular. The Glyphs panel allows you to select exactly the glyph you need.

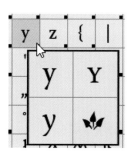

Photoshop's type-handling capabilities have expanded considerably since the emergence of both the web and social media, but some things are not as easy to find as they might be. When you need a special character or symbol, where do you go? You wouldn't necessarily think of searching for the Glyphs panel – but that's exactly where you should be heading.

1 To insert a glyph, position your Text Insertion Point where you want the glyph to appear. Choose Type > Panels > Glyphs Panel to show the Glyphs panel.

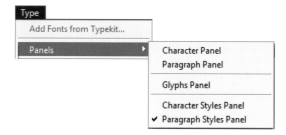

2 It's a good idea to make the Glyphs panel bigger when you first start to use it, to make it easier to find the glyph you are looking for.

3 Select a font family from the Font Family pop-up menu. Scroll through the list of glyphs.

4 Double-click the glyph you want to use. The glyph appears at the Text Insertion Point and also appears in the Recent Glyphs section at the top of the panel.

Understanding the Glyphs panel

Select a font and weight from the Font Family pop-up menu – each font has a set of glyphs specific to itself. Different fonts may have different glyphs available.

Recently used glyphs appear in the top row of the Glyphs panel.

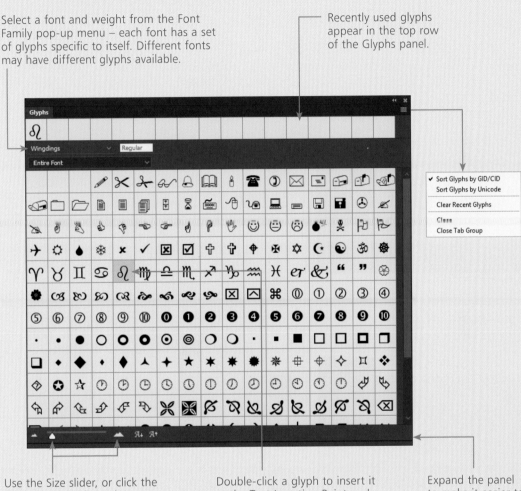

Use the Size slider, or click the Scale Down/Scale Up buttons to make the glyph thumbnails larger or smaller.

Double-click a glyph to insert it at the Text Insertion Point and to add it to the Recent Glyphs at the top of the panel.

Expand the panel to make it easier to find the exact glyph you are looking for.

Use the Alternates pop-up to narrow down your search to a specific category of glyphs.

Wood and stone carving

This tutorial demonstrates a straightforward way to create a carved wood type effect without using too many complex layer styles to achieve the result. This is a quick and easy way to work your type into a wooden surface.

The technique uses pixel-based layers rather than editable type layers, as this allows a slightly random effect as well as control over the opacity and blend mode of different layers. It uses two layers with layer effects applied and some optional burning of some of the edges of the type.

1 Use the Type tool to create the text you want to work with. Create settings you require for the type – use a serif font, typical of traditional carved inscriptions; use a bold or black weight so that the layer styles have space to take effect.

2 In the Layers panel, hold down ctrl/cmd and click the type layer to load a selection in the exact shape of the type. Click the Visibility button ( ) to hide the type layer.

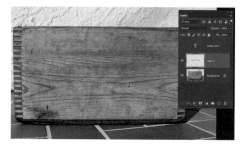

3 Click on the Background layer to select it. Choose Layer > New > Layer via Copy (ctrl/cmd + J) to create a copy of the type, made up of pixels, to the new layer.

4 Hide the Background layer to see the result of copying the type selection to the new layer.

5 Make sure the type pixels layer – Layer 1 in this example – is active. Select the Burn tool. Set an Exposure of 40-60% in the Options bar. Leave the Range pop-up set to Midtones. Using the Burn tool, randomly darken areas of the type pixels, then concentrate more burning on the left edge of each letterform.

6 Create a Layer Style for Layer 1 – the pixel type layer. Click the fx button ( ) at the bottom of the Layers panel. From the style options list on the left, select the Bevel & Emboss checkbox. Change the Style pop-up to Emboss. As a starting point, use the settings in the screenshot (opposite), but be prepared to experiment with settings – the choice of type size and font, along with the texture of the wood surface, all have an influence on the result. You need to create settings that work for your specific combination. Click OK when you are satisfied with your settings.

In these screenshots, for comparison purposes, "out" does not have any burning applied to it.

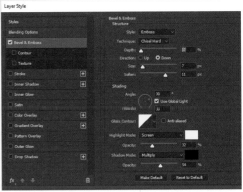

7 Make a copy of Layer 1. Now, double-click the Bevel & Emboss label to show the Layer Style dialog box with the settings for Layer 1. Change the Style pop-up to Pillow Emboss. Create the settings for the effect indicated in the screenshot. As for the first layer, be prepared to experiment to find the right settings for your combination of elements.

8 Adjust the opacity of Layer 1 to adjust and fine-tune the effect. You can also experiment with Blend modes for Layer 2, using the Opacity slider to soften and reduce the strength of the Blend mode to finalize the effect.

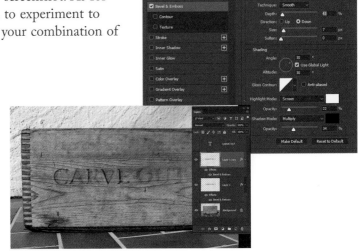

...cont'd

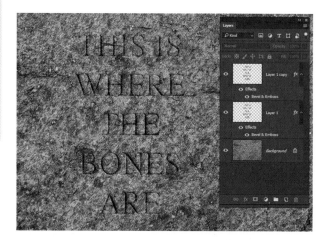

Stone carving

You can use a similar range of techniques, with a few variations, to create a stone-carved effect. Again, variables such as the background texture, font and type size mean that you will need to vary some of the settings to achieve the end result you require.

1 Start by creating your type layer. Create a selection using the type layer. Copy pixels from the Background layer to a new layer. In this example, don't use the Burn tool to randomly burn or darken areas of the type on Layer 1.

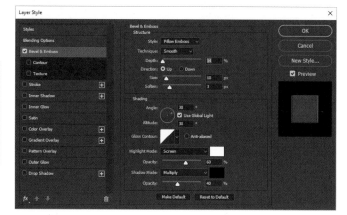

2 Layer 1 in this example is a Pillow Emboss layer style. Use the settings in the screenshot as a starting point.

3 Layer 1 copy is an Inner Bevel layer style. Again, use the settings in the screenshot as a starting point.

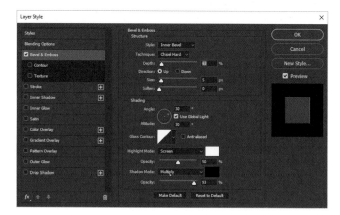

Neon type

Neon type – it's one of those versatile effects that can bring an interesting dimension to an image. There are endless variations on how to achieve the effect – this technique uses two main type layers, several layer styles and a couple of filters, and is an example of how layer styles and filters can combine to create interesting, visually stimulating effects, adding impact and atmosphere.

It's worth making a copy of the original editable type layer, so that you can easily edit and re-work the effect at a later stage.

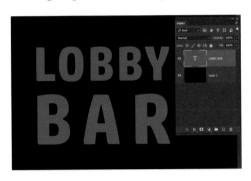

1 Neon type works best on a dark textured background – typically, brickwork works well, but you can also try concrete textures. Create the text you want to use. This example uses HP Simplified, Bold, 123 point. Color is Red = 250, Green = 10, Blue = 190.

Be prepared to vary and experiment with settings. The results you get will depend on the type size, color and font, and background that you combine as you build the effect.

2 With the type layer selected, begin by adding four layer styles: Drop Shadow, Inner Glow, Inner Shadow, Bevel & Emboss. Click the fx button at the bottom of the Layers panel, then select an option to show the Layer Styles dialog box, or choose Layer > Layer Style. Use the settings in the screenshots (in the colored panel on page 108). Each layer style is editable, so you can go back and change and tweak settings at various stages as you build the effect.

The first time you set up the layer styles, it is worth setting each one in turn, then OK the Layer Style dialog box so that you get an understanding of exactly what each effect brings to the final result.

3 The letterforms need to have an inner area of white to create the tubing effect. To achieve this, choose Layer > Rasterize > Type to convert the editable type to pixels. Ctrl/cmd + click the newly rasterized type layer to create a selection of the pixels on the layer. Choose Select > Modify > Contract. Use a setting of around 14 pixels. Press either Delete or Backspace to remove the inner areas of the type so that they become transparent.

When you're ready, you can set up all the layer styles at the same time simply by clicking on each Layer Style checkbox, then clicking the label (e.g. Inner Glow) to show the settings:

...cont'd

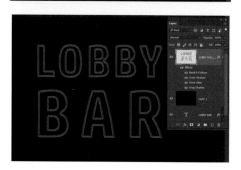

4. The next step is to create the appearance of white tubing. Ctrl/cmd click the rasterized type layer to again select all the pixels on the layer. Choose Select > Modify > Contract. Enter a value of around 3-4 pixels. OK the dialog box. Choose Edit > Fill. In the Fill dialog box, select White from the Contents pop-up. Click OK to fill the inner areas of the selection with white, to create the white tubular effect.

5 Now it's time to create the neon glow. Make a copy of the rasterized type layer: choose Layer > New > Via Copy (ctrl/cmd + J), or drag the layer down onto the New Layer button at the bottom of the Layers panel. Select the bottom type layer, then remove all existing effects from the layer by dragging "Effects" onto the Trash button at the bottom of the panel.

6 To create the glow, (on the bottom type layer) choose Filter > Convert for Smart Filters to allow re-editing and re-working of the settings at any point. Choose Filter > Blur > Gaussian. Enter a value of around 12 pixels, then click OK to create the initial glow. Choose Filter > Blur > Motion Blur. Enter an angle of 16 degrees and an amount of 36 to add a degree of further distortion to the initial Gaussian blur.

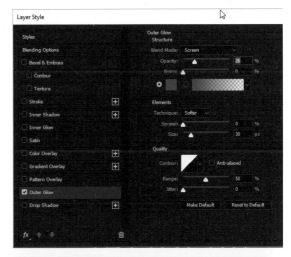

7 Finally, add a layer style to the glow type layer. Click the fx (fx) button at the bottom of the Layers panel. Select Outer Glow. Start with the settings indicated in the screenshot, then experiment with your own to achieve the final result.

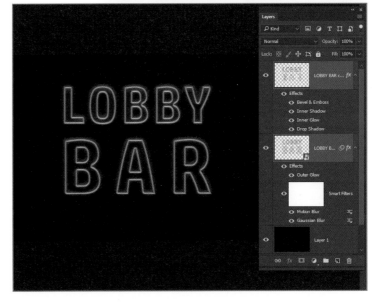

109

Type on circles logo

Here's a tutorial that brings together a range of text-handling techniques with techniques for working with type, paths and shape layers.

Remember to select a path in the Paths panel, and click on the path name. To select the path in your artwork, select the Path Selection tool ( ), then click on the path. To deselect and hide a path, click in an empty area of the Paths panel – below any of the existing paths.

1 Drag in a vertical and horizontal ruler guide to create a center point around which you can build and align the various paths and layers required to create the effect.

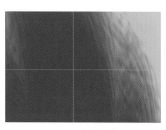

2 Select the Ellipse Shape tool (from the Shape tool group). In the Options bar, make sure the Type pop-up is set to Path.

3 Position your cursor on the center point of the guides, start to press and drag, to draw a path, then hold down Alt/option to draw from the center out, then hold down Shift to constrain the path to a perfect circle. Release the mouse button before you release the Alt/option and Shift modifier keys, so that you don't lose the constraining effect of the Shift key.

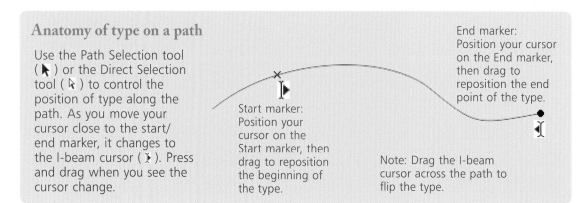

Anatomy of type on a path

Use the Path Selection tool ( ) or the Direct Selection tool ( ) to control the position of type along the path. As you move your cursor close to the start/ end marker, it changes to the I-beam cursor ( ). Press and drag when you see the cursor change.

Start marker: Position your cursor on the Start marker, then drag to reposition the beginning of the type.

End marker: Position your cursor on the End marker, then drag to reposition the end point of the type.

Note: Drag the I-beam cursor across the path to flip the type.

4 Notice in the Paths panel that you now have a Work Path.

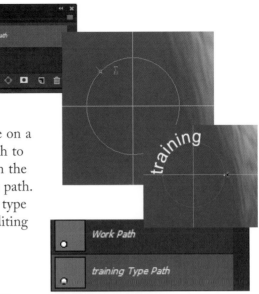

5 Select the standard Horizontal Type tool. Position your cursor on the path – notice it changes to the Type on a Path cursor ( ). Click to convert the path to a new type path – again, you can see this in the Paths panel. Start typing to add text to the path. Notice, in the Layers panel, a new editable type layer. You can use standard highlighting, editing and formatting techniques to work on the appearance of your text.

6 To control where text sits on the path, select the Path Selection tool. For type on a circle, it can be useful to drag the start and end markers to the midpoint position on each side of the circle. Select center alignment to center the text along the top edge of the circle.

Create type at the bottom of the circle

1 In the Paths panel, you should still have the original Work Path. Click on it to select it. If you don't see the original Work Path, repeat Step 3 on page 110 to draw a new circular path, centered on the guides, and to the same dimensions as the original circle.

Hot tip

To avoid confusion it can be useful at this point to hide the previous type layer you just created.

2 Select the Type tool, position your cursor on the path, and again click to place the Text Insertion Point on the circle. Enter the text you want to appear at the bottom of the logo design.

3 Repeat Step 6 above to position the start and end markers at the midpoints of the sides of the circle.

...cont'd

Think of the start and end markers as the left and right margins of the type on a path.

4 This time, for type at the bottom of the circle, select the Path Selection tool. (The type path should still be selected in the Paths panel.) Drag the midpoint marker bar around the circle to reposition the type at the bottom. Drag the I-beam cursor ( ) across the path of the circle to flip the type.

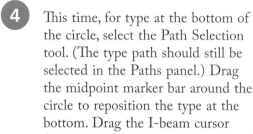

5 To get the type to work effectively, you typically need to adjust the tracking and baseline shift of the type.

Create a background circle to reverse out type

1 To create a circle to back the type, select the Ellipse Shape tool again. This time, select Shape from the Type pop-up in the Options bar. Using a shape layer to create a background circle for the type makes it easier to adjust and fine-tune using the Properties panel. The new shape layer

appears above the currently active layer – change the layer stacking order later on to move it below the type layers.

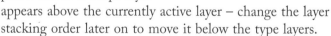

2 Use the Properties panel to change the fill to None and to create a thick stroke with the color you want.

3 Fine-tune all type settings and the thickness and color of the circle.

6 Transform, Reflect, Shadow and Light

This chapter brings a taste of some the myriad possibilities that Photoshop provides for creating, manipulating and transforming elements. Master these controls, and the creative possibilities are endless.

Perspective transformations

This sequence uses some low-resolution assets. It starts with a fairly low-resolution canvas size, so that the imported assets don't need to be scaled up too much to work at the resolution of the destination document.

You can easily transform objects, layers and type. Here's a quick exercise that uses the Perspective transform manipulation to create a simple 3D space that you can use for further transformation work to practice other techniques covered in this chapter.

This walk-through builds in many of the other techniques covered in this book, so that you get a feel for how effective you can be when you master a range of the advanced shortcuts and controls available in Photoshop.

1 Choose File > New and select the Print option to set up a new document. In this example, the document is set up at 150 ppi as it uses some low-resolution assets at 72 ppi. Width and height is 8.268 by 5.827 inches, Artboards off, RGB color mode, White as the background.

2 Choose View > New Guide to set up a vertical guide at the center point of the canvas. Select Vertical and enter a value of 4.134 inches (105 millimeters).

3 Use the Rectangle Shape tool. Make sure the Type pop-up in the Options bar is set to Shape.  Draw a rectangle – this will be the back wall of the 3D space. Position the drawing cursor on the vertical guide, hold down Alt/option, then drag to draw from the center out. The rectangle is now centered on the vertical guide.

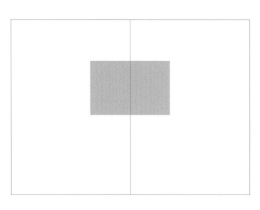

4 Use the Properties panel to create a fill color – make sure that Stroke is set to None, Fill to 35% Gray.

...cont'd

5 Select the Move tool (V). Position your cursor on the back-wall rectangle. Hold down Alt/option. Notice the cursor changes to the copy cursor. Drag to the left to create a copy of the original rectangle. Use the smart guides that appear automatically to make sure it snaps to the right edge of the original and aligns perfectly. This creates a copy of the original rectangle a on new layer. It's worth naming each new layer as you create it.

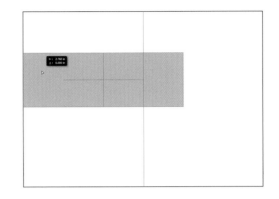

6 Use ctrl/cmd + T to access the free transform bounding handles for the layer. Position your cursor on either the top-left or bottom-left corner bounding box handle. Hold down ctrl/cmd + Alt/option + Shift, then drag the handle, to invoke the perspective transform. Drag vertically upwards to create the left wall of the 3D space. Click the Commit transform button when you are satisfied with the result.

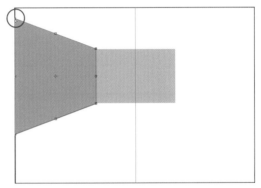

In this sequence, the room layers are named and referred to as: back wall, left wall, right wall and ceiling.

7 In the Layers panel, double-click the layer thumbnail for the left wall to show the Color Picker panel. Select a slightly different shade of gray. Click OK.

8 Hold down Alt/option, then drag copy the left wall to the right so that its right edge snaps onto the right edge of the original back wall.

...cont'd

9 Free transform the layer – this time, position the cursor slightly outside the transform bounding box. When you see the rotate cursor (↻), hold down Shift, drag in a circular direction and rotate the object through 180 degrees.

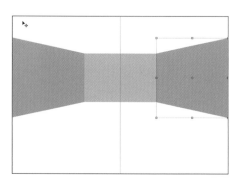

Remember to name your layers as you create them:

10 Then, move it to the right, so that its left edge snaps to the right edge of the back wall. Commit the transformation. Again, recolor the right wall.

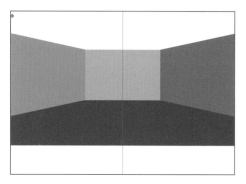

11 Use the Rectangle Shape tool, set to shape, to draw a large rectangle to form the floor area.

12 Use the Properties panel, which should pop up automatically, to change the color.

Move layer to bottom of layer stack

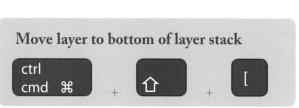

ctrl
cmd ⌘   +   ⇧   +   [

13 Be generous with the width of the rectangle – this will allow you the option of off-centering the 3D space later on, if desired. Use the keyboard shortcuts ctrl/cmd + Shift + [to move the shape layer to the bottom of the layer stack.

...cont'd

14 Use ctrl/cmd + J to make a copy of the floor layer. Position your Move cursor on the shape on the canvas, then drag upward: it will start to appear above the walls. Hold down Shift as you drag, to constrain the movement vertically so that it doesn't move left or right.

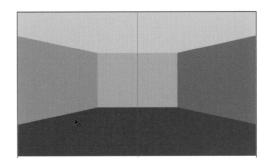

15 Five shape layers come together using various transformations and layer changes to create a very simple 3D space.

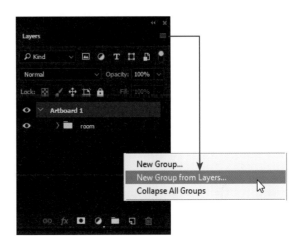

16 Use ctrl/cmd + Alt/option + A to select all layers. Then, from the Layers panel menu, select the New Group from Layers command to move the room layers into a new layer group.

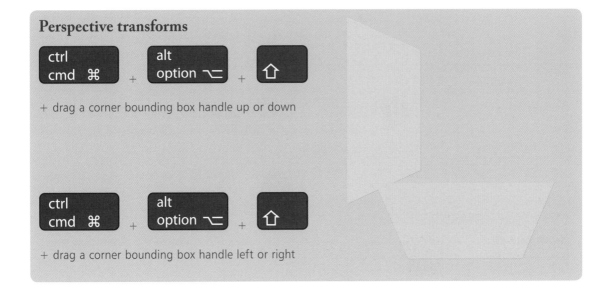

Perspective transforms

| ctrl cmd ⌘ | + | alt option ⌥ | + | ⇧ |

+ drag a corner bounding box handle up or down

| ctrl cmd ⌘ | + | alt option ⌥ | + | ⇧ |

+ drag a corner bounding box handle left or right

Create a reflection

Reflections work best if there is either a textured or gradient background to provide some variation in the result. This example uses a simple gray-to-white gradient in the background, and a claw hammer with the background removed.

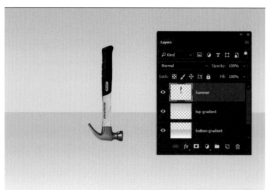

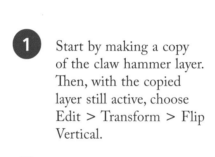

1 Start by making a copy of the claw hammer layer. Then, with the copied layer still active, choose Edit > Transform > Flip Vertical.

2 Select the Move tool, and drag the flipped copy downward, so that it butts up against the base of the original hammer. With the Move tool selected, you can use the up or down cursor keys on the keyboard to nudge the copy up or down to create the final position.

Hold down Shift as you drag the layer to constrain the move to vertical, so that the object remains perfectly aligned with the original.

3 Move the copy layer below the original layer. Either drag the layer down manually, or use the keyboard shortcut indicated below.

4 Shorten the overall length of the copy so that it is a slightly more compressed version of the original. Use Free Transform, then drag the center-bottom bounding box handle upward.

Move layer down in layer stack

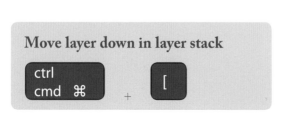

5 With the copy layer still active, create a layer mask. Either click the Add Layer Mask button () at the bottom of the layers panel or choose Layer > Layer Mask > Reveal All. A white layer mask thumbnail appears to the right of the layer thumbnail. All pixels representing the claw hammer remain visible.

6 Use the Gradient tool on the layer mask to gradually fade out the bottom of the handle selected. Select the Gradient tool. From the Gradient Picker select the Black/White gradient. Position the cursor roughly halfway down the handle of the copy. Drag upward on the image to create a black-to-white gradient on the layer mask, which fades the handle into the background.

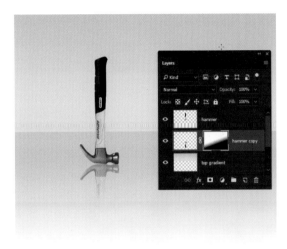

7 Be prepared to experiment with Blend modes for the layer to create an interesting and realistic result. Color Burn in this example creates a slight glossiness to the reflection that works well with the surface. Also, you can use the Opacity slider to reduce the opacity and allow some of the background to show through the effect.

8 As a finishing touch, you could use the Burn tool on the reflection layer to darken the area at the base of the original object. Make sure the layer thumbnail is selected, not the layer mask thumbnail.

Reflect, transform, blend and mask

This tutorial introduces two more transformation techniques to cast a more complex reflection than the one covered in the previous sequence.

 One of the biggest advantages of using Smart Objects is that you can perform non-destructive edits to the Smart Object. For example, you can change your mind about resizing a Smart Object without fear of losing resolution and reducing quality.

1 Bring your window into the 3D room space. Choose File > Place Linked to place the window as a Smart Object.

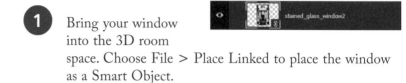

2 Choose Edit > Free Transform to show the transform boundary box handles. Position your cursor on a corner handle, hold down ctrl/cmd + Alt/option + Shift, then drag vertically to create a perspective transform.

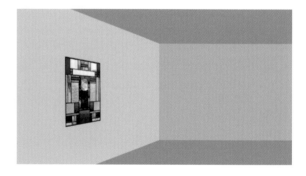

3 Press the Enter key, or click the Commit button in the Options bar, to accept the transform when you are ready.

Create reflection

Creating a reflection of an object in perspective is a little bit more complex than the reflection in the previous example.

1 Create a copy of the window layer. Use ctrl/cmd + J or choose Layer > New Layer > Via Copy.

2 Creating the reflected copy of the original stained glass window requires a combination of techniques. You can do them in the order that works best for you. Start with a vertical flip; choose Edit > Transform > Flip Vertical.

3 Rotate the layer by -90 degrees. Then use the Free Transform tool, hold down ctrl/com, and drag a corner handle to create a sheared effect. Do this to the corner handles as required. Be aware that the shape will grow when you blur it, but you can also use free transform on the blurred layer content later if required.

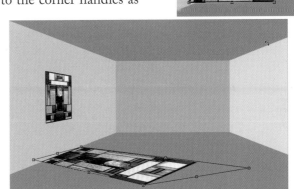

Shear transforms

 + drag a center-top/bottom bounding box handle left or right

 + drag a center-left/right bounding box handle up or down

...cont'd

Blend the reflection to the background

When you apply a filter to a Smart Object, Photoshop automatically converts the layer to a Smart Filters layer so that you can edit filter settings at any time as required:

1 Use Filter > Blur > Gaussian and set a value of 10 pixels. Depending on the underlying layer, experiment with settings to get the best result.

2 Set the layer Blend mode to Screen, and adjust the layer Opacity to 67%. Be prepared to experiment with the Blend mode, depending on the background you are blending into.

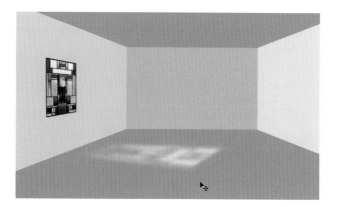

Unconstrained transforms

ctrl
cmd ⌘

+ drag a corner bounding box handle

Transform Again and Copy

Transforming a layer in Photoshop – scale, rotate, move and skew – are simple, basic operations. Here's a technique that takes transformations to the next level – it builds on the technique of Transform Again.

1 Using Ruler Guides, create a center point for the transformation to work around.

2 Create a shape you want to rotate around the center point. It's useful if the object is centered on the vertical guide, but not essential.

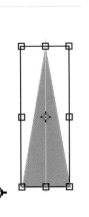

3 Working with the Move tool, and with the layer selected, choose Edit > Transform > Rotate. Or, use the keyboard shortcut, ctrl/cmd + T. The transform bounding box appears around the object. Most importantly for this technique, the Reference Point marker appears, initially at the center of the transform bounding box.

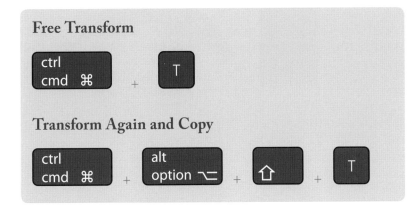

Free Transform

ctrl cmd ⌘ + T

Transform Again and Copy

ctrl cmd ⌘ + alt option ⌥ + ⇧ + T

Provided that you have dragged the Reference Point marker from its original position, and provided that it remains selected, you can enter values in the X/Y entry fields in the Options bar to position the reference point accurately.

...cont'd

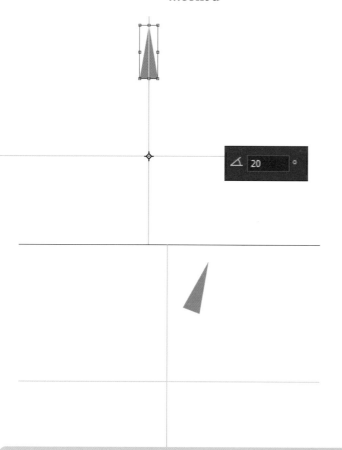

4 Position your cursor on the Reference Point marker. Drag this to the intersection of the ruler guides you placed earlier, in Step 1 – the center point for the rotation.

5 Enter a value in the Rotate field in the Options bar – typically any value that divides neatly into 360; for example, 15, 30, 36. The larger the value, the further apart each copy will be.

Reference Point marker

One of the keys to working with transformations is the Reference Point marker (◈). The Reference Point marker is the fixed point around which a transformation takes place. As well as dragging this to a new position (as in the example outlined above), you can also control the initial position of the marker using the proxy reference point matrix in the Options bar.

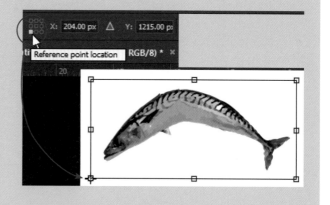

Alternatively, when you initiate a transformation, before you do anything else you can simply click elsewhere to reset the Reference Point marker at a precise, custom location.

...cont'd

6 Accept the transformation.

7 Use the keyboard shortcut, ctrl/cmd + Shift + Alt/option + T to repeat the same transformation on a new, copied layer.

In the mackerel example above and around, the Transform and Copy Again command is used on an object that was moved, rotated and resized.

8 Repeat the keyboard shortcut to continue making new copies, a new layer for each copy, of the object with the same transformation settings applied.

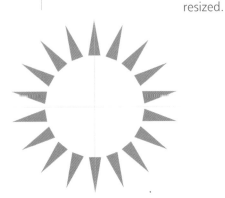

Lots of layers

Using the Transform and Copy Again technique outlined here, you're likely to end up with a lot of layers in your Layers panel. To make your Layers panel and the artwork you are working on more manageable, you could select all the duplicated layers, then choose New Group from Layers, in the Layers panel menu (▤), to group all the related layers together whilst keeping each duplicate as a separate layer **1**; or, you could choose Merge Layers (ctrl/cmd + E) from the Layers panel menu to consolidate all the duplicates into a single layer **2**. Which option you choose depends on the flexibility you need.

Beams of light

To add some more photo realism to the stained glass window, the next element that is needed is a beam of light. The illusion of light is difficult to re-create – the aim of this example is to do enough to convince the viewer to supply the understanding and imagination to achieve a successful effect.

1 Create a new layer above all existing layers. Name it "beam" to make it easily identifiable.

2 Use the Polygonal Selection tool to create a selection that defines the extent of the beam you want to form.

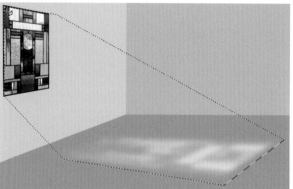

The Polygonal Selection tool creates a selection formed by straight line segments. You can hold down Alt/option then drag the mouse to define a freeform portion of the selection, if required.

3 Choose Select > Modify > Feather. Enter a value of 24 pixels. As always, be prepared to experiment with settings, depending on the requirements of the image, its resolution, and the effect you want to create.

4 With the layer still selected, click the Curves adjustment layer button in the Adjustments panel. In the Properties panel, click at the center point and drag up and to the left to brighten the area. Reduce the opacity for the layer to reduce the impact of the curves adjustment to a more realistic level.

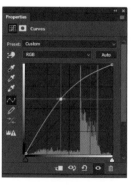

5 Reform the selection again: hold down ctrl/cmd and click the layer mask thumbnail then, click back on the new layer you created to make it active.

6 Select the Gradient tool. From the Gradient Picker select the Transparent Rainbow gradient. Drag diagonally across the window area from the bottom-left to the top-right corner.

When you use a gradient that includes transparency on a layer mask, unlike a gradient using solid colors, if you use the Gradient tool more than once, each time you drag you add to the existing gradient, rather than replacing the previous gradient.

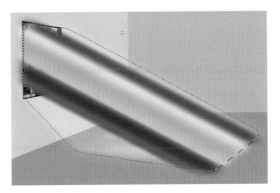

7 Change the Blend mode for the layer – in this example, to Screen. Reduce the opacity for the layer. Create a layer mask, and use a black-to-white gradient to blend the rainbow gradient effect to an acceptable level.

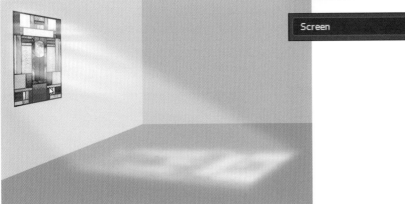

Casting shadows

Import an image of a chair, or any other object for that matter, into a scene that it's not from originally, and there's every chance that it will look as if it's an uninvited guest, or like a poor-quality bunch of plastic flowers – artificial and unrealistic. Add a reasonably realistic shadow, and suddenly it starts to blend into its new surroundings.

1 You need a shadow to blend the chair into the scene with a degree of realism – without a shadow the chair looks artificial and sticks out like a sore thumb. To start, make a selection of the chair.

2 Create a new layer for the shadow to give more flexibility and control. Make sure the layer remains selected. Fill the selection, on the new layer, with black.

3 Rotate the shadow 180 degrees – either manually, or choose Edit > Transform > Rotate 180°. Move the layer below the chair layer. Reduce the Opacity of the layer – this can be fine-tuned later, as you go along.

4 Transform the shadow using a combination of shearing – by dragging a center-top, bottom, left or right bounding box handle whilst holding down ctrl/cmd – and

unconstrained distortion using ctrl/cmd and dragging a corner handle.

You can readjust the layer opacity at any time as necessary to achieve the final result.

5 Notice how shadows fade and lose strength as they move further away from the object. Add a layer mask to the shadow layer. Use a black-to-white linear gradient to create a fade on the shadow. (See Chapter 3 – Layers and Masks – for further information.)

6 Depending on the underlying surface and the strength of the shadow, using a Blend mode can help create a more realistic effect. (See Chapter 4 – Layer Blend Modes – for further information.)

Notes on shadows

Learn from the shadows – ever-present – around you. They vary enormously, depending on many factors – the strength and position of light source, the position and size of the object, the reflectiveness and texture of surfaces. They tend to get narrower the further away they get, and they also spread and lose density.

Along with transforming shadows to a realistic shape, the other controls that can be useful when forming shadows are a layer mask with a black-to-white gradient to gradually fade out the shadow, a Gaussian blur to make the shadow less sharply defined, and often, a Blend mode and reduced opacity settings to help meld the shadow into its surroundings.

The Create Layer command

It's very often the shadow that helps blend an image into another image, creating the illusion that elements originating in one image belong in a different image. The shadow you create does not have to be perfect, but you can go a long way to making it realistic, and so achieve a convincing and effective final result.

As with many tasks in Photoshop, there's the need for realism and accuracy to be balanced with the need for speed. When it comes to creating a realistic shadow quickly, the Create Layer command is an excellent way to achieve this balance.

1 Let's get started with the image of a plant pot on top of a wooden box opposite. The aim is to blend this content into a different image and in doing so create a realistic and effective shadow.

2 This technique starts with a cutout of the wooden box and plant pot on a layer, and another layer – the white

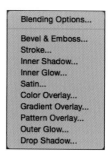

background – which makes it easier in the first instance to see the effect of the tips and tricks included in this exercise. There will be a few finishing touches carried out in the destination image where the cutout and shadow end up.

3 Make sure the cutout layer is selected. At the bottom of the Layers panel, click the Add Layer Style button (**fx**). Select Drop Shadow. (You can also access this command by choosing Layer > Layer Styles – you'll need to be aware of this sub-menu for later in this sequence.)

An Effects layer can consist of multiple layer styles that combine to produce the final result.

4 Create the settings you want for the standard drop shadow. Start by using the settings in the screenshot opposite if you are using the training

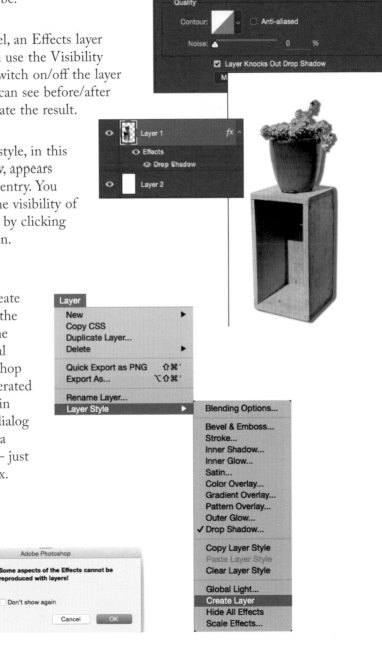

file. If you are using your own image, experiment with your own settings. Click OK. This gives you a basic drop shadow – but it's not very realistic or effective in this situation and it's not as lifelike as it could be.

5 In the Layers panel, an Effects layer is created. You can use the Visibility button ( ) to switch on/off the layer effect so that you can see before/after versions and evaluate the result.

6 The specific layer style, in this case Drop Shadow, appears below the Effects entry. You can also control the visibility of the Drop Shadow by clicking its Visibility button.

7 Choose Layer > Layer Style > Create Layer to separate the layer effect into the separate, individual layers that Photoshop automatically generated from the settings in the Layer Styles dialog box. You may get a warning window – just OK the dialog box.

...cont'd

8 Take a look at the result in the Layers panel – the original cutout layer no longer has an integrated Effects layer; the drop shadow is separated out onto its own layer. Notice that the Fill slider in the Layers panel probably indicates a reduced value below 100%. Also, Multiply is set as the layer Blend mode.

9 You are now in a position where you can manipulate the drop shadow to make the shape more realistic, and add some blending options to help it integrate with the destination image more effectively.

Manipulating the separate shadow layer

1 Make sure Layer 1's Drop Shadow layer is selected. Transform the shadow using a combination of shearing, by dragging a center-top, bottom, left or right bounding box handle whilst holding down ctrl/cmd, and a Free Transform distortion using ctrl/cmd and dragging a corner handle. (See pages 114-122 for information on transforming objects and layers.)

2 You may also need to move, rotate and resize the shadow to achieve the shadow you want.

Manually painting parts of the shadow

You may find that manipulating the extracted layer style shadow doesn't

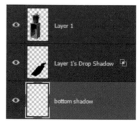

quite create the final shadow effect. In this example, there needs to be a thin shadow under the front lip of the box, and a slightly wider shadow running along the side.

1 Again, for flexibility and to be able to re-work settings, create a new layer on which you can paint the required shadow. Position the layer below the Layer 1 Drop Shadow layer and the box/plant.

2 Select the Brush tool. Set a soft edged brush and use the [and] keys to create a suitable brush size. Make sure the Foreground Color is set to black. Click on the left, at the base of the box, hold down Shift – to create straight line segments – and click at the base on the right of the box. Keep Shift held down, and click at the back corner of the box.

You can add a Gaussian blur and a layer mask to make the shadow more and more realistic.

3 Change the layer opacity to match the larger shadow area and change the Blend mode for the layer to Multiply – the same as the extracted Drop Shadow layer.

Move shadow and cutout layers to the destination

1 Select the plant layer, and both the shadow layers, then click the Link Layers button (🔗) at the bottom of the Layers panel so that you can drag all three layers into another destination document at the same time.

2 Drag one of the linked layers onto the filename tab of the destination image when the destination image becomes active. Without releasing the mouse button, drag into the destination image window, then release the mouse.

Generating scripted patterns

Scripted patterns bring an interesting extra dimension to what you can achieve with patterns. Each scripting option – Random, Brick, Cross Weave, Spiral and Symmetry – provides comprehensive controls for creating intricate patterns quickly and easily.

The following instructions indicate specific measurements and settings – experiment with settings, colors etc. to create your own unique results.

1 Create a new document. The document in this example is 400 x 400 pixels, 96ppi and RGB.

2 Either create a new layer for greater flexibility and control, or work on the Background layer.

3 Choose Edit > Fill, then select Pattern from the Contents pop-up:

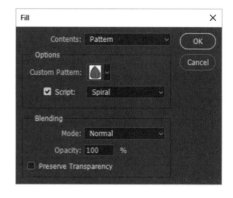

4 Select the pattern object you want to use from the Custom Pattern pop-up.

5 Select the Script check-box. Then, select an option from the Script pop-up.

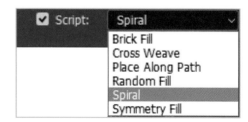

6 Use the dialog that appears, to create settings for the specific script option:

...cont'd

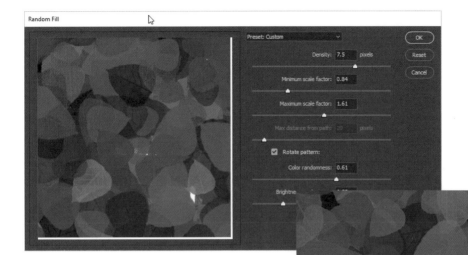

7 OK the dialog box when you are satisfied with your settings.

Filling objects with a scripted pattern

Scripted patterns can be useful in a variety of ways. Here's an example of how you can fill a cushion or any other soft furnishing to create interesting and varied textures.

1 Create a selection of the objects you want to fill.

2 Use ctrl/cmd + J to copy the selection to a new layer:

3 Make sure the contents of the layer are selected. Hold down ctrl/cmd and click the layer thumbnail in the Layers panel if necessary, to select all pixels on the layer. Choose Edit > Fill.

...cont'd

4 Select the pattern object you want to use from the Custom Pattern pop-up.

5 Select the Script check box. Then, select an option from the Script pop-up. Click OK.

6 Use the dialog that appears, to create settings for the specific script option.

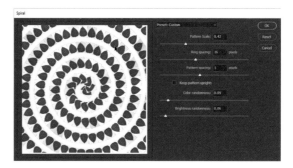

7 OK the dialog box, to fill the selection with a scripted pattern:

8 Try changing the Blend mode and Opacity settings for the layer to achieve the final result you require.

Fill dialog box

⇧ + F5

7 Path Power

Speed, flexibility, accuracy

– there are times when it's

only the Pen tool and the

ability to manipulate points

and paths that can deliver

the precise, accurate results

you require.

Paths and shape layers

The more tools you have at your disposal, the easier it becomes to implement and develop your creative ideas, and the more you can achieve. There is nothing more frustrating in Photoshop than having a brilliant idea, then failing to realize it because you lack the tools and control to bring it to life.

Master the Pen tool in Photoshop, and you have mastered the Pen tool in Adobe Illustrator and InDesign – yet another excellent reason to make the Pen tool a key tool in your arsenal.

You can create and manipulate paths using tools in the Pen Tool group, together with the Path Selection and Direct Selection tool.

You can also create shape layers using tools in the Shape Tool group – with the Type pop-up in the Options bar set to Path.

Understand paths and start to use and control them, and you add an essential and powerful toolbox of techniques and possibilities that can facilitate and enhance your creativity.

And remember also that shape layers are vector shapes formed by editable paths, so that, for example, it's often convenient to start with a basic shape such as a circle, then edit the path so that it becomes a different shape, as in the example below.

Use the Convert tool to convert the center-top and center-bottom anchor points to corner points. Use the Direct Selection tool to move both points downward. Still using the Direct Selection tool, manipulate the direction points for each of these anchor points to create the final shape.

But, don't go any further until you understand the terminology – you need to know your anchor points from a direction handle, and a direction point from a line segment. Look for and recognize the interface detail – it tells you so much about what is about to happen as you use the various tools. (See the colored panel opposite.)

Key concepts – paths and points

Paths

A path defines the shape of an object – it's a geometric construct. A path can be made up of straight line segments, curve segments or a mixture of both. Curve and line segments are joined together by anchor points.

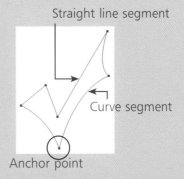

Straight line segment

Curve segment

Anchor point

Anchor points – selected or not selected

It's very important when you start to create and manipulate paths that you can identify whether or not an anchor point is selected.

Selected = solid square

Not selected = hollow square

Straight line segments

Curve segments

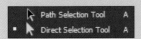

Use the Path Selection tool to select the entire path, to move it, resize it etc. as a complete object.

The Direct Selection tool is the primary tool for manipulating the shape of a path. You use it to select/deselect anchor points and their associated direction lines and direction points. Once selected, you can use the Direct Selection tool to reposition the anchor point, and to control the shape and length of the curve or line segments using the direction points.

Direction line

Direction point

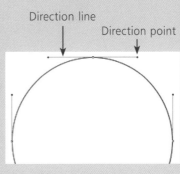

Drawing smooth curves

This demonstration shows you how to draw smooth curves using the Pen tool, and introduces some general techniques that you can use whenever you are using the Pen tool and Direct Selection tool to create and perfect paths.

When you start to use the Pen tool to draw curves, move the cursor a relatively short distance – short jumps – before you set the next anchor point. With practice, as you get more and more proficient using the Pen tool, you'll find that you can typically set anchor points further apart. In general, the fewer anchor points you create, the smoother the curves you create. Be slightly less adventurous to start with, and you'll find that you have better control over the paths you create.

1 Make a mental note of where you start to draw your path – this makes it easier to complete the path when you come back to the beginning.

2 Position your cursor on the edge of the object you want to trace around and cut out or select.

3 Click. This sets the first anchor point. Move your cursor to a new position along the shape where you want to create the next curve segment. Do not press and drag the mouse – simply move it to the next position along the shape.

4 Press and drag the mouse. Drag in the direction of the shape you want to cut out. (Keep to the outline of the shape you are tracing – try not to let the cursor wander to either side of the shape; keep it following the outline of the shape.)

This action, pressing and dragging, does two things. First, it sets the shape of the incoming curve segment – the curve between the first anchor point and the one you are setting. This part of the curve is controlled by the direction point that appears (moving backward in the direction of the preceding anchor point).

The second thing it does, as you drag forward in the direction of the shape you are tracing, is that it sets the direction point that will control the shape of the outgoing curve segment (in conjunction with the next anchor point you create).

5 Repeat the process. Move the cursor to a new position – remember, this is not a press and drag. At the new position, where you want to set the next anchor point, press and drag. As you drag, try to match the incoming curve segment to the shape of the object you are tracing, and keep the outgoing direction line following the curve of the object you are tracing.

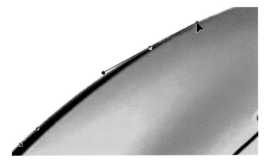

Here's an example of something you want to avoid when drawing curves. Pressing and dragging away from the anchor point, but not following (more or less) the shape or contour of the object, doesn't set an accurate incoming curve segment, and the next anchor point you create is unlikely to create a smooth curve segment that conforms to the shape.

Incoming/outgoing curve segments and direction points

The placement of the incoming direction point controls the shape of the incoming curve segment (indicated by the gray line segment as you draw), and the placement of the outgoing direction point will influence and control the shape of the next curve segment you draw.

...cont'd

Try to keep the direction lines quite short, and the outgoing direction point following the outline of the shape you are tracing around.

Don't worry if you make a mistake, or the curve you are creating doesn't appear to be totally accurate. You can fine-tune and re-work the path into its final shape after you complete the first pass using the Direct Selection tool together with the Convert Point tool. (See page 151 for further information.)

6 Keep setting anchor points and curves to define the shape of the object until you get back to the start point. When you place your cursor on the start anchor point, notice that a small circle appears at the cursor to indicate that you are about to complete the path. Either click to close the path, or in this case, press and drag – yet again in the direction of the object shape, to complete the path.

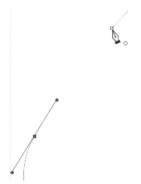

7 Notice that a Work Path entry appears in the Paths panel. This is a temporary path – you can only have one work path in a document at a time. Select Save Path from the Paths panel menu (▤) to make the path permanent.

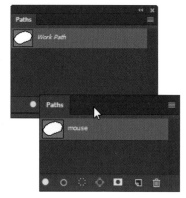

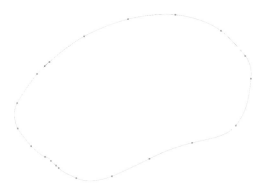

Drawing straight line segments

Drawing straight line segments is one of the more straightforward techniques for drawing a path in Photoshop.

1 Select the Pen tool, then click to place the first anchor point.

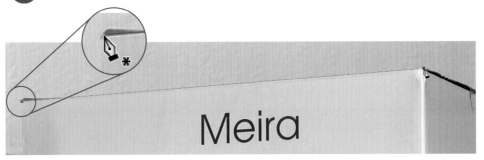

2 Move your cursor to a new position – where you want the line segment to end. (This is not a press and drag.) Then click to set the anchor point.

3 Repeat the process: move, then click; move, then click; as many times as required.

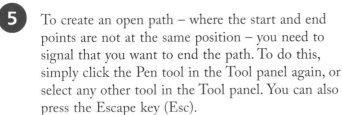

4 Notice the small circle that appears at the cursor when you position your cursor back over the start anchor point. Click to create a closed path.

5 To create an open path – where the start and end points are not at the same position – you need to signal that you want to end the path. To do this, simply click the Pen tool in the Tool panel again, or select any other tool in the Tool panel. You can also press the Escape key (Esc).

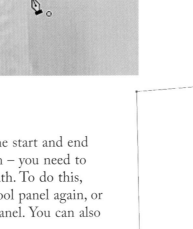

A work path is a temporary path. You can only have one work path in a Photoshop document. Save a work path if you want to keep it and make it permanent.

Selecting paths and points

To work effectively with points you must first be able to show or hide the path. You can then use the Path Selection tool to select the entire path, and the Direct Selection tool to select and manipulate the anchor points as well as curve and line segments.

Showing and hiding paths

1 To select a path, it must first be showing. To show a path, click on the path name or Work Path in the Paths panel.

Path not selected

Path selected

2 To hide a path, in the Paths panel click on some empty space below the path entries to deselect it. Or press Escape on the keyboard.

For selections that are difficult and sometimes time-consuming to make with the selection tools, the Pen tool provides a powerful alternative, especially for making highly accurate selections.

After you create a work path, you can click the Load path as selection button to convert the path to a selection:

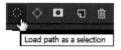

To select an entire path

1 Make sure the path is showing.

2 Select the Path Selection tool. Click on a path in your artwork to select it. All the anchor points that form the path become solid.

3 Drag any part of the path – an anchor point, line segment, or curve segment – to reposition the entire path. You can also press the arrow/cursor keys on your keyboard to nudge the path in small increments.

4 Click away from the path, on some white space, to deselect it.

To select anchor points

1 Make sure the path is selected in the Paths panel.

2 Select the Direct Selection tool. Click on an anchor point to select it. If you click on a curve point, the associated direction points and direction lines appear. The individual anchor point turns solid.

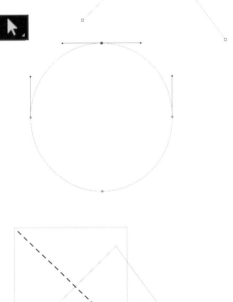

3 If you click on a curve or straight line segment, the segment is selected and the associated direction lines and points for that segment appear, but the anchor point remains unselected – hollow.

4 With the Direct Selection tool, drag to create a rectangular selection marquee (the dotted line) to select multiple anchor points.

5 Click away from the path, into some white space, to deselect the path.

Vector shapes

Paths are mathematically defined vector shapes consisting of lines and curves. They are "resolution independent", which means that working in Photoshop, when you scale them up (or down) they retain a crisp, mathematically accurate shape that does not lose resolution, and therefore quality, if you make them bigger.

Mixed straight and curve segments

When you need to create paths consisting of a mixture of straight line and curve segments, things can become more complex and slightly trickier to begin with. But, take a little time to practice, learn and master the following techniques, and you'll be amazed at how proficient and effective you can become.

Remember, you can always return to the path after you finish drawing and make final adjustments using the Direct Selection tool, at a later stage.

Straight to corner to straight

Here's a fairly common scenario, a straight line segment that then needs go into a curve segment to go around a smooth corner, then back to a straight line segment.

1 Working with the Pen tool, click to place the first anchor point.

2 Move your cursor to the beginning of the corner you need to trace around. Click to end the straight line segment.

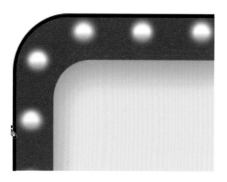 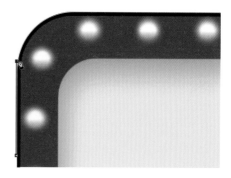

Hold down Shift, in Step 5, before you click, if you want to constrain the line segment to vertical or horizontal.

3 Move your cursor to the end of the curve, where you want the next straight line segment to begin. Press and drag to define a smooth curve. Keep the mouse button pressed down whilst you focus on getting the incoming curve segment as accurate as possible. Release the mouse button when you are satisfied.

4 Hold down Alt/option and click the anchor point you just created in the previous step. This removes (retracts) the outgoing direction point. This is the essential step that makes it easy to continue with a straight line segment.

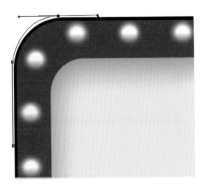 

5 Move your cursor to a new position – click to set a new anchor point and create a straight line segment to the new anchor point.

Fix as you go
Whenever you are drawing paths, if you are unhappy with the position of an anchor point or the shape of a curve after you create it, you can hold down ctrl/cmd to access temporarily the Direct Selection tool. Use the Direct Selection tool to make edits to the points. When you release the ctrl/cmd key you can continue to add more points to the path.

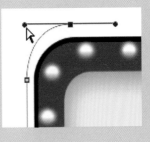

Smooth points to corner points

When you can transition from a smooth point to a corner point and back, you'll find that most objects become much easier to trace around and cut out.

Again, be prepared to practice this technique a few times – it will pay dividends – you'll soon be the master of the paths you create: instead of the paths controlling you, you will control the paths.

You need corner points to create a sharp change of direction at the anchor point. Sometimes, curve points simply don't fit the bill.

Smooth points to corner points

1 Working with the Pen tool, press and drag, as normal, to create the smooth point preceding the point that needs to be a corner point. The corner point is where you need a sharp change in direction at the anchor point, which cannot be achieved using a smooth point. Release the mouse button when the incoming curve segment is accurate and the outgoing direction point follows the shape of the object.

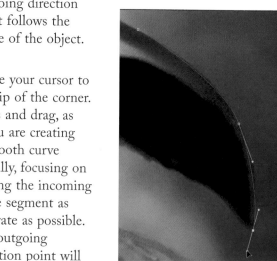

2 Move your cursor to the tip of the corner. Press and drag, as if you are creating a smooth curve initially, focusing on getting the incoming curve segment as accurate as possible. The outgoing direction point will not be following the direction of the object at this moment in time. Do not release the mouse button.

3 When you are satisfied with the incoming curve segment, hold down Alt/option and drag the outgoing direction point to follow the shape of the object. This is the essential step in this sequence. Holding down the Alt/option key before you release the mouse button frees up the outgoing direction point so that it no longer balances the incoming direction line. You now have complete, independent control over the outgoing direction point – and its position has no effect on the incoming curve.

4 Release the mouse button when you have positioned the outgoing anchor point along the outline of the object you are tracing.

5 Move your cursor to a new position; continue to create further smooth or corner points as required.

The Convert Point tool

Hidden in the Pen Tool group is potentially one of the most powerful precision tools in Photoshop. The Convert Point tool is essential for the precise fine-tuning of the paths you create in Photoshop.

All the Convert Point tool functions work in exactly the same way in Adobe InDesign and Adobe Illustrator.

What you have to be very careful about, and fully understand, is whether you are targeting a direction point or an anchor point, and whether the technique requires you to click or to press and drag the mouse to achieve the desired result.

To begin with, to avoid confusion, it is best to perform one action with the Convert Point tool, then return immediately to the Direct Selection tool to make further edits. The initial confusion that can arise with the Convert Point tool is that if you perform more than one action with the tool, you can inadvertently undo the previous edit. (See the colored panel below for an example of how things can go wrong.)

Convert smooth point to corner point

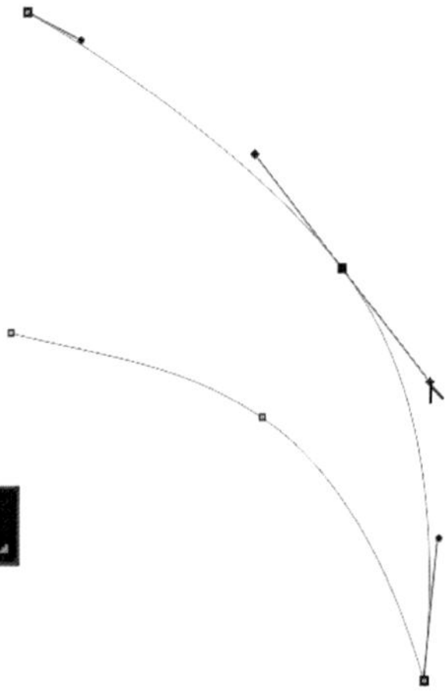

1. Make sure the path is showing in Paths panel. Use the Direct Selection tool to select the path. Click on the smooth anchor point you want to convert. Its direction points should appear.

2. Select the Convert Point tool. Position your cursor on a direction point ( ), then press and drag. The smooth anchor point now

(continued on page 152...)

Where it can go wrong

For example, if you use the Convert Point tool to convert a smooth point to a corner by dragging a direction point, but then still using the Convert Point tool, you try to drag the anchor point to a new location, you actually convert the corner point back to a smooth point.

Understanding smooth and corner points

You can use the Direct Selection tool to edit anchor and direction points and also to identify whether an anchor point is a smooth or curve point. A smooth point guarantees a smooth transition of the curve through the anchor point. A corner anchor point allows for a sharp change of direction at the point. Most paths you create in Photoshop use a mixture of both point types, which is why understanding their behavior and mastering them is so important.

Smooth

When you drag a direction point in a circular direction, the opposing direction point moves to always maintain a position diametrically opposed to the point you move – a bit like a see-saw, both direction lines are always in a straight line. You can, however, change the length of one of the direction lines without affecting the length of the other direction line.

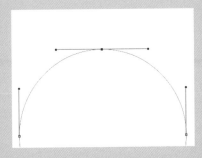 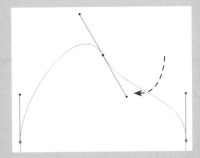

Corner

When you drag a direction point in a circular direction, the opposing direction point is not affected. You have complete, independent control over each direction point. This is what allows you to create a sharp change of direction at the anchor point.

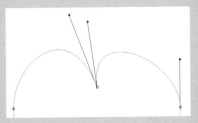 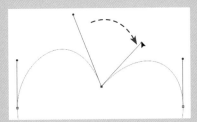

...cont'd

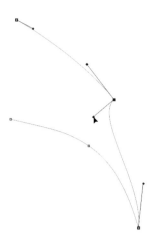

becomes a corner point. You can manipulate either direction point without affecting the other related point. This is what allows you to create a sharp change of direction – a corner point.

Convert a corner point to a smooth point

You can continue to use the Convert Point tool to make changes to the Direction points. But, if you click or drag the anchor point you will undo the corner point conversion. If you want to make further edits to the shape of the path, do so using the Direct Selection tool.

1 Using the Direct Selection tool, click on a corner anchor point to select it. The associated direction lines and points appear.

2 Select the Convert Point tool. Position your cursor on the anchor point. Drag on the anchor point to create a symmetrical smooth point: the direction handles are equidistant from the anchor point, and balance each other – move a direction handle in a circular direction, and the opposing handle moves so that both are always in a straight line.

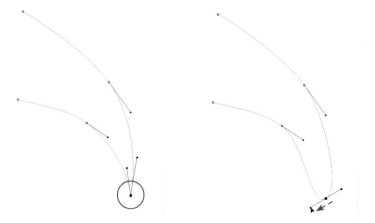

3 Select the Direct Selection tool to make any further edits to the direction points or anchor point.

Retract direction points

1 Make sure the path is selected. Select the Convert Point tool, then position your cursor on either a smooth or corner anchor point.

2 Click on the anchor point to retract both direction points.

When you have the Convert Point tool selected, it is only when you position your cursor on an anchor point or a direction point that the cursor changes to the Convert Point cursor (⌐). If you move the cursor over other parts of a path, it appears as the Direct Selection tool cursor – the white arrow (⌐).

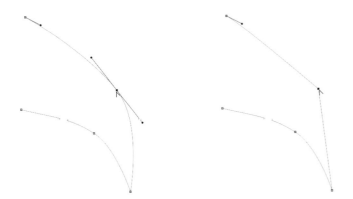

3 To retract an individual direction point, using the Convert Point tool, very carefully drag the direction point onto the anchor point. You need to be really precise to get this technique to work.

Create a symmetrical curve point

1 Make sure the path is selected. Select the Convert Point tool, then position your cursor on either a smooth or corner anchor point.

2 Drag on the anchor point to create a symmetrical curve at the anchor point – where the direction handles are equidistant from the anchor point and balance each other. This technique works on any anchor point – smooth, corner or retracted.

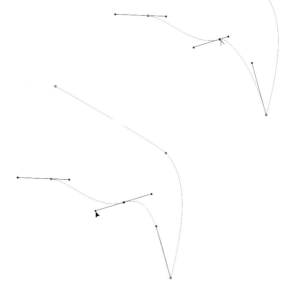

Load All Shapes

Custom shapes provide a library of useful vector shapes that can become the basis for further customizations using the Direct Selection tool. The default set of shapes is useful, but there are additional sets of shapes available. You can load additional sets individually, or for convenience, it can be worthwhile loading all custom shape sets.

1 Select the Custom Shape tool from the Shape Tools group. Click the Shape pop-up in the Options bar to show the default shapes.

2 Click the Settings button (⚙) to access the custom shape sets pop-up menu. Click an individual set name. In the warning prompt dialog box, click OK to completely replace the default set with the set you selected, or click the Append button to retain the existing custom shapes and add the new set.

You can go back to the original set of default shapes only, at any time: click the Settings button in the Custom Shapes picker, then select Reset Shapes:

Reset Shapes...
Load Shapes...
Save Shapes...
Replace Shapes...

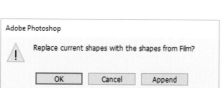

3 To have quick access to all shape sets, select All and click Append in the warning prompt. It's then worth expanding the Custom Shapes panel so that you can quickly and visually identify the shape you want to work with, without having to scroll up and down through a long list of shapes.

8 Cloud Power

New cloud-based services provide enhancements to Photoshop that deliver efficiencies and creative opportunities.

Creative Cloud (CC) Libraries

Creative Cloud Libraries make reusing assets easy, and bring collaborative opportunities to the creative process.

CC Libraries are easy to set up, easy to use, and provide efficiencies and enhancements to the way you work in Photoshop. You can store, access, manage and reuse graphics, color palettes, layer styles, brushes and character styles – essentially, all the elements you use on a regular basis and that you might want to locate and implement quickly – across multiple PCs, Macs and other devices using the same Adobe ID, as well as for collaboration across teams.

If consistency and efficiency are words central to your Photoshop creative workflow, then CC Libraries is an aspect of Photoshop you need to exploit.

You can create as many libraries as you need – for example, to accommodate different clients, specific projects or particular categories of artwork.

When you are adding elements to a CC Library, you can add individual attributes, such as a color or a layer style, or you can add multiple attributes that are applied to the layer you are working with:

You need to be connected to the internet to create a CC Library in the first instance. Once created, you can work with items in your Libraries without being connected. If you edit any of the elements in a Library whilst offline, the changes you make are synced back to the cloud version when you next go online and use Photoshop.

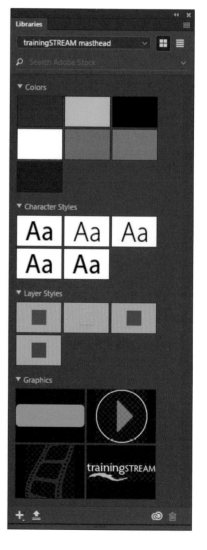

A screenshot of a CC Library panel that contains all the standard, repeating elements of the trainingSTREAM website masthead. When you move your cursor onto the panel, name labels appear for each of the elements as you hover over them.

To create a new Library

1 Show the Libraries panel – choose Window > Libraries if it is not included in the Panel dock.

2 Click the Library pop-up, then select the Create New Library button ( ).

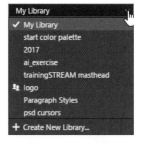

3 In the Create New Library panel that appears, enter a name in the Create New Library entry field.

4 Click the Create button to create the Library and add it to your other Creative Cloud Libraries. You can now start to populate the Library with the elements you want to reuse.

Working with colors

1 To add a color to the active Library, make sure the color is set as the Foreground Color.

2 Click the Add pop-up button () at the bottom of the Library panel. In the pop-up panel, make sure the Foreground Color checkbox is selected. Click the Add button.

...cont'd

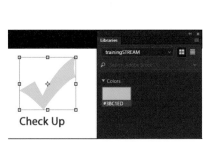

3 To apply a color from a CC Library, expand the Colors section of the Library if necessary, make sure you have a Shape layer or a Type layer selected, then click on a color swatch in the CC Library.

 To apply a color from a CC Library to a pixel-based layer, with the layer active, right-click (Win) or ctrl + click (Mac), on the color swatch in the Library, then select Apply Color Overlay, to apply the color as an effect. This does not apply the color directly to the pixels, but rather creates a color overlay for the pixel on the layer:

Working with Character Styles

1 Apply character formatting to a type layer – this becomes the model for the Character Style you save to the CC Library. Make sure the Type layer remains active.

2 In the Libraries panel, click the Add pop-up button (⊞). In the pop-up panel, make sure the Character Style checkbox is selected. Click the Add button.

3 To apply a Character Style from a CC Library, make sure a type layer is active, then click on the Character Style in the Libraries panel.

Working with Layer Styles

1 Apply a Layer Style in your artwork – this becomes the model for the Layer Style you save to the Library. Make sure you keep the layer active.

2 In the Libraries panel, click the Add pop-up button (➕). In the pop-up panel, make sure the Layer Style checkbox is selected. Click the Add button. The Layer Style is added to the Layer Styles category in the Library.

3 To apply a Layer Style from a CC Library, make sure you select the layer to which you want to apply the Layer Style, then click on the Layer Style in the Libraries panel.

Remember, the Add pop-up is context-sensitive – the options available depend on the properties of the active layer.

List View/Thumbnail View

Click the View buttons to move between Thumbnail View and List View. List View can be useful, as it displays more information in the readouts.

Working with graphics in Libraries

Adding graphics – Shape layers or pixel-based content layers – to a Library is straightforward, but there are more options when you place a graphic from a Library. You can place graphics as either linked objects or as embedded objects.

You have the option to add the Fill or Stroke colors applied to a graphic as separate Library elements at the same time as you add the graphic.

1 Make sure the layer you want to add to the Library as a graphic is active.

2 Click the Add pop-up button (**+**). In the pop-up panel, make sure the Graphic checkbox is selected. Click the Add button.

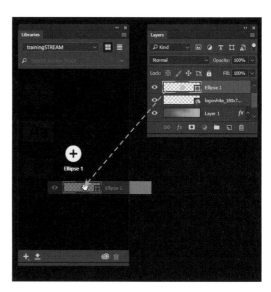

3 Alternatively, you can drag the layer from the Layers panel into the Libraries panel. Release when you see the "+" icon.

Placing graphics from a Library

1 Drag the graphic from the CC Library into your artwork. A bounding box appears around the graphic. You can use the bounding box handles to resize the graphic.

Position your cursor inside the bounding box, then drag to reposition the graphic.

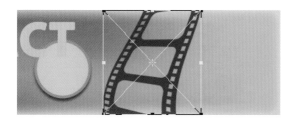

2 When you are ready to accept the graphic, either click the Commit button in the Options bar, or press Enter/Return on the keyboard.

3 When you drag a Library graphic from the Libraries panel into your artwork, the graphic appears on a new layer immediately above the currently active layer. A CC Library icon appears in the corner of the layer to indicate that this graphic is linked to the original in the CC Library. This is a linked graphic – it is not an embedded Library element.

4 Hold down Alt/option as you drag a graphic element from a Library to embed the graphic in the Photoshop document. This graphic does not need to link back to the original – the artwork is embedded within the Photoshop document.

Editing Library graphics

Double-click on a graphic in a CC Library to open the graphic as an individual element in a new Photoshop window. You can now edit the object – for example, you might change its color or shape. Save and close the Library element to update the object in the Library. Where linked objects exist in Photoshop files, they will update to reflect the changes to the master Library object when you next open the Photoshop file.

New Library from Document

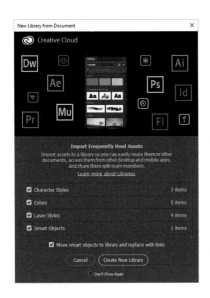

When you open a Photoshop document that includes Character Styles, custom colors, Layer Styles or Smart Objects, the New Library from Document dialog box opens.

This gives you the option of using the document to automatically create a CC Library that can act as a template to define settings and graphics, colors and layer styles that you can reuse conveniently and consistently across an entire project.

This can be a major time saver if you are creating a series of related graphics, for a website or an app, where any number of the elements will remain the same, and where you need a library of elements that can be deployed consistently whenever needed to establish and maintain a brand or a theme.

Graphic objects

Smart objects

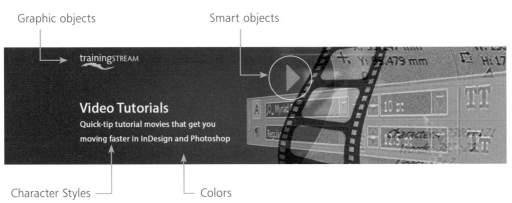

Character Styles

Colors

1   In the New Library from Document dialog box, use the checkboxes for Character Styles, Colors, Layer Styles and Smart Objects to select which elements, in the document you are opening, should be included in the CC Library.

2 Click the Create New Library button.

3 Photoshop uses the name of the document as the name for the Library. You can change this as required.

4 Use the Expand/Collapse triangle (▶) to the left of each category to show/hide the contents of the Library.

Rename a CC Library

1 From the Libraries panel menu, choose Rename.

2 Enter a new name in the Rename entry field, then click the Rename button:

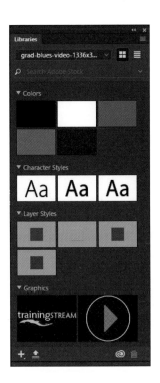

 You can add additional colors, character styles, layer styles and graphics to the Library at any time – the New Library from Document command provides a quick and convenient automated starting point.

Use the elements extracted by the New Library from Document command to ensure consistency across any number of related documents in the same project. And, add any additional elements as required to make the Library an invaluable project resource that will, in numerous instances, save you from reinventing the wheel.

163

Irritated by the New Library from Document dialog box popping up?

If it irritates you that the New Library from Document dialog box appears – select the Don't Show Again checkbox at the bottom of the dialog box. Now, as an alternative procedure, you can click the New Library from Document button at the bottom of the Libraries panel (⬆) to achieve the same result whenever you need it – you are not faced with the New Library from Document panel every time you open a document that includes custom colors, layer styles, smart objects or character styles.

Collaborating with Libraries

Using Libraries to collaborate means that teams can work more effectively and consistently. All members of a collaborative library can make changes to the items in the Library as well as adding and deleting items – updates made by any collaborator sync back to the original master Library.

1 To set up a Library for collaboration, choose Collaborate from the Libraries panel menu (▤). Photoshop launches your browser, loads **assets.adobe.com**, and displays the Invite Collaborators panel.

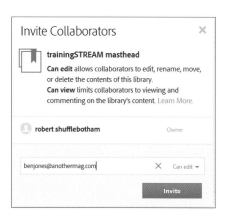

2 Enter the email address of the colleague you want to invite to the Library. Use the pop-up menu to set access privileges for the Library.

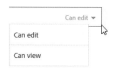

3 Continue to add email addresses and access privileges as required, then click the Invite button.

Receiving and accepting invites to collaborate

1 To accept an invitation to collaborate in a Library, the invitee can either click the accept the invitation link in the invitation email, or alternatively, they can accept the invite via the Creative Cloud panel.

An invitation to collaborate in a Library can also be accessed via the Creative Cloud panel.

2 The invitee can then accept the pending invitation and, optionally, view the Library online in a web browser. Their Libraries panel updates with the Library if they have Photoshop open, or the next time they launch Photoshop.

A collaboration icon appears next to the collaborative Library.

3 Any edits to existing items or additions/deletions are synced back to the master Library so that all collaborators can see and have access to the changes – including the owner of the Library.

You're in charge

When you set up a Library for collaboration, although collaborators can edit, add and delete items from the common Library, you are still the "owner" of the Library – you can at any time decide to remove collaborators and deny access to the Library. Simply click the Invite People button in the web console, then either Remove all users or individual collaborators.

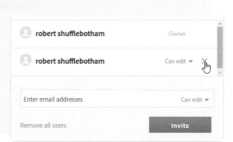

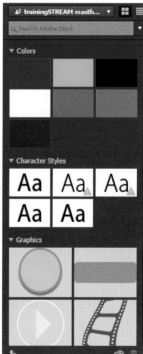

Sharing links to Libraries

Beware Changes made to a shared Library that is a copy do not update the original. Also, updates made to the original CC Library by the owner do not update in a follower's Library.

Hot tip Add a description if you want to make the recipient aware of any issues or important information relating to the use of the Library.

Don't forget If you no longer need access to a shared CC Library that you are following, choose Unfollow <name of Library> from the Library panel menu (▤).

Sharing links to CC Libraries is a powerful way to include other team workers in your project and to keep them informed and up to speed with developments. You can make a Library available for viewing read-only in a browser, or you can allow another user with an Adobe ID to download their own copy of the Library for use in Photoshop, InDesign and Illustrator.

1 To share a link to a Creative Cloud Library, select Share Link from the Libraries panel menu (▤). This opens **assets. adobe.com** in your browser and displays the Send Link dialog box. Click the Private/Public toggle button (⊙) to share a read-only version of the Library.

2 Copy the shortened URL. Specify which Additional Options you want to implement for the share. Click the Save button. You can now email the shortened URL to another team member.

Accessing the shared link

1 The recipient can click the shortened URL or copy and paste it to their browser to display the Library contents as a web page.

2 If the recipient has an Adobe ID, they can click the Follow button. By signing in, they can access the Library from their own Libraries panel in Photoshop, InDesign and Illustrator.

Typekit

Typekit is Adobe's online font library service, providing access to a growing selection of high-quality fonts. In the early days of digital design and publishing, an abundant choice of "top class", professionally designed fonts would have been an expensive luxury – limited to major publishing companies and design agencies.

Managing fonts between designers, clients and printers, not to mention Mac and PC platforms, was difficult, time-consuming and, as a result, costly and inefficient.

With Adobe's launch of Typekit, the considerable costs and quite significant organizational challenges have become things of the past. Make use of Typekit in your projects, and wave goodbye to creative limitations in your use of type. It's up to you to exploit the possibilities.

Typekit gives you a vast array of choices for type that would previously have been an expensive luxury.

With Typekit, you gain access to a huge variety of professionally designed fonts. Many are free, although there are also fonts that you must license and pay for.

Downloading Typekit fonts

1 To download and sync a font from Typekit – for use not only in Photoshop, InDesign and Illustrator, but also for other common applications such as Microsoft Word – choose Type > Add Fonts from Typekit.

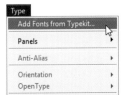

2 Alternatively, with the Type tool selected, click on the Font pop-up in the Options bar, then click the Add fonts from Typekit button.

3 The Adobe Typekit website launches. Browse the font cards to find a font you want to sync for use on your computer desktop in Photoshop and all other Adobe desktop applications.

4 Click on a font card to go to the Font download page. The total number of fonts available for the typeface are indicated on the right-hand side.

...cont'd

5 Scroll through the font weight and style listings to find the ones you are interested in. Click the Sync button to download and sync the font to your computer.

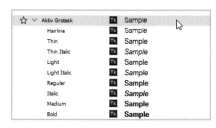

6 Fonts from the Typekit font library display the green Typekit icon (**Tk**), making them easy to identify.

Filtering Typekit fonts

1 Click the Show Typekit filter button, available from the Font pop-up menu in either the Options bar or the Character panel, to show only the Typekit fonts synced to your computer.

2 The button is a toggle – click it again to remove the Typekit filter.

If you have already synced a font for use on your desktop, the Sync button changes to UNSYNC with a message to indicate that the font is synced:

UNSYNC

Font is synced

Adding Typekit fonts using the Creative Cloud app

You can also add Typekit fonts from the Creative Cloud desktop app. Select Assets, then Fonts, then click the Sync Fonts from Typekit button to sync and manage Typekit fonts.

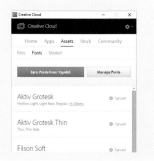

Managing Typekit fonts

You have a Typekit Portfolio plan included in your Creative Cloud subscription – typically, there is a limit of 100 fonts that you can sync for free at any one time. Fonts that are free or available to buy (with the free-of-purchase status) are indicated on the Font cards that you browse on the Typekit website. When you are on a specific font page, fonts that are free to sync have a green Sync button; fonts available for purchase have a shopping cart button and a price.

 You can check how many fonts are included in your Creative Cloud subscription, and how many you have already synced, by clicking the Account button on the Typekit Homepage:

 👤 Account

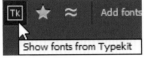

Unsyncing fonts

1 To unsync a font, launch the Creative Cloud Desktop app.

2 Select Assets, then Fonts. Click the Manage Fonts button.

3 Click the Unsync button for the font to remove it from your computer.

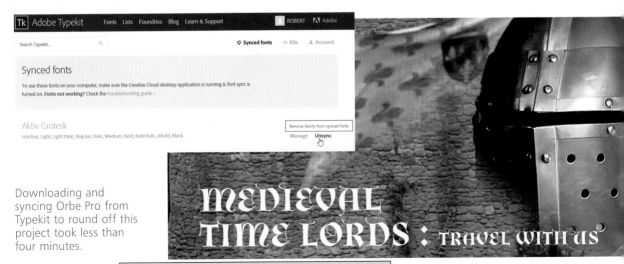

Downloading and syncing Orbe Pro from Typekit to round off this project took less than four minutes.

Behance it

Read the Terms and Conditions before you publish your work on Behance.

Behance is another powerful and convenient cloud service that is included in your Creative Cloud subscription. Behance is an online platform where you can publicize and showcase your creative work. Sign in to Behance using your normal Adobe ID, then create project showcases.

1 From Photoshop, choose File > Share on Behance. This takes you to **behance.net**, where you can log in using your Adobe ID.

2 Click the Add Work button to load the Project Editor.

Add Work

3 Click the Upload files button to upload files directly from your desktop. You can also load files from your Creative Cloud assets and from Lightroom.

4 When you are ready, click the Continue button.

Click the Preview button to evaluate the uploaded content before you go ahead and make the project visible on Behance:

Preview

5 Click Step 2 Cover to choose a cover image for the project and to scale and crop it as required. You can also give the project a title. Click the Crop and Continue button to move to Project Settings.

6 Create Project Settings to provide relevant information and to make your project discoverable.

7 Click the Save button to save uploaded files and settings you've created if you are not ready, at this point, to make your project public. Click the Publish button to make the project public on **behance.net**

Save   Publish ▸

9 Actions and Output

Actions – it's a significant area of Photoshop often overlooked by even seasoned Photoshop professionals. Actions are versatile, powerful, and above all, flexible. Quick Export As and Export As take your ability to deliver on time, flexibly, for print or screen, to a new level.

Action stations

Large parts of layout and design are about consistency, accuracy and speed. In many publishing projects, whether this is for print or the web/screen, there is often a high degree of repetition required to achieve the consistency and accuracy needed to create a coherent, convincing and persuasive final product.

An action is an automated set of commands that you can run on an image or series of images. They save you time, as you don't have to repeat steps manually to perform a fixed series of steps on your image.

If you want to become a power user of Photoshop, you need to take a look at Actions. Actions are one of the biggest time savers in Photoshop, and at the same time, one of its most neglected features.

The Actions panel is one of those panels that can be a bit off-putting at first, but brings huge rewards if you spend a little time to master it. Like with so many of the more advanced functions in Photoshop, begin with some simple, basic routines to get started, and then add layers of complexity as your understanding, mastery and confidence grows.

Create a set

Start by creating your own set so that you can easily locate and identify the custom actions you set up.

1. Choose Window > Actions to show the Action panel.

2. If necessary, click the Expand/Collapse button (▶) to the left of Default Actions label to hide the display of the preset actions.

3. Select New Set from the Actions panel menu (▤). Enter a name for the set, then click OK. This gives you a new

set where you can group related actions together, or action sets for specific projects. You are now ready to create your first action.

Create an action

The basic steps for creating an action are straightforward, and apply to all the actions you create. Follow the steps on the next page to set up a specific action.

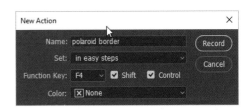

1 Open an image that you can use as the initial model for creating the action.

2 Make sure the set you created is active. From the Actions panel menu (▤) select New Action. Or, click the Create new action button at the bottom of the Actions panel.

3 In the New Action dialog box, enter a descriptive name for the action you are about to record. If necessary, from the Set pop-up, select the correct set where you want to save the action. Click OK. You are now ready to record the steps you want save as an action. Notice the Begin Recording button (⬤) at the bottom of the panel turns red.

4 The action's name appears in the panel and the red Recording in Progress button (⬤) appears.

5 Proceed to record commands (detailed on the next pages) in the sequence you want them to be replayed. Click the Stop Recording button (■) to end the recording.

You don't need to rush when you set up an action – there is no sense in which the clock is ticking; it's not the same as an audio or video recording.

Polaroid effect

Here's an example of an action that creates a Polaroid-like border around an image. The idea is to apply this same effect to a series of 20-30 images, which might then be used in a print layout, or online, depending on the resolution of the images you are working with.

1 Create a new action as outlined on page 173, then click Record to record the following steps.

2 Working with a sample image, double-click the Background layer. The New Layer dialog box appears. You can leave the name as it appears – Layer 0. Click OK in the dialog box. The result is that Layer 0 is no longer a default Background layer and you can now move other layers below it, which you cannot do for a Background layer.

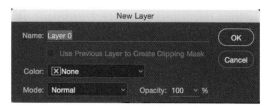

3 Next, extend the canvas area around the image. Choose Image > Canvas Size (cmd/ctrl + Alt/option + C). Change the measurements pop-up to Percent. Click the center-bottom placement square to control where the extra canvas area is added – in this example, above and to the left and right. Enter the values in the screenshot and

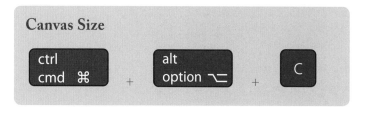

then OK the dialog box to add an extra 5% canvas area for the left, top and right edges.

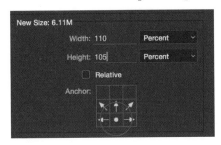

4 Use Canvas Size again – this time to set a wider area at the bottom of the image. Again, take a look at the settings in the screenshot.

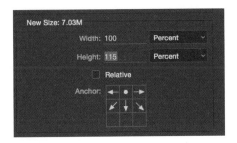

5 Create a new layer in the Layers panel. This appears above the existing layer – Layer 0. Choose Edit > Fill. In the Fill dialog box, select White from the Contents pop-up menu. OK the dialog box.

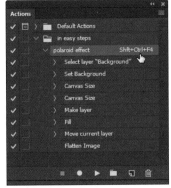

6 Drag Layer 1 below Layer 0 in the Layers panel. Or, use the keyboard shortcut (ctrl/com +]).

7 In the Layers panel menu (▦), select Flatten image.

8 Click the Stop Recording button in the Actions panel.

9 Close the image without saving changes. Reopen it and play the action to test it.

In this example, the drop shadow is applied as an effect in InDesign, but it would be easy enough to record extra steps to add more canvas area and then a drop shadow effect to build the drop shadow into the Photoshop action.

Do it quicker

If you've taken the time to create an action, you'll also want to run your action in the quickest and most convenient way. When you set up an action, take the time to set up a keyboard shortcut from within the New Action dialog box. (If you've already set up actions without setting a keyboard shortcut, you can go back and edit the action.)

Keyboard shortcuts for actions use the "F" keys, along with either Shift, cmd/ctrl or both Shift and cmd/ctrl together.

Note, if you assign an action the same shortcut that is already used for another command, the shortcut applies the action and not the command.

Adding commands to an action

Sometimes you create an action and realize some time later that you'd like it to include additional commands that you didn't think of when you initially created it. Rather than re-create the action with the new commands from scratch, it's usually much more efficient to edit and enhance the original.

1. Open an image so that you can make judgments about any of the settings you are about to create.

2. In the Actions panel, make sure the action you want to edit is expanded so that you can see each individual command in the sequence.

3. When you record a new command it appears after the currently selected command. Click on a command to select it and to specify where the new command appears – in this example, after Set Background.

4. Click the Record button (◉). Use the commands and create appropriate settings to edit the action. In this example, add a new Black & White adjustment layer – Max Black from the presets pop-up and select the Tint checkbox.

5. You can add multiple new commands if you want to.

6. Click the Stop Recording button (◼). Close down the image without saving changes. Reopen the same image and play the action to check that it works as intended.

Playing and controlling actions

When you are ready to run an action, you can run the complete action on an image, or you can be selective, and run only certain commands in the action. You can also stop actions at specific commands so that you can customize settings in dialog boxes in order to treat each image individually. These options are some of the ways you can control actions to bring flexibility, control and efficiency to your work with actions.

Excluding specific commands from an action

Notice when you first set up an action, every checkmark in the "run" column on the left of the panel is active – a light-gray color. There may be times when you want to run an action, but omit certain steps for that occasion.

Drag command entries up or down in the Actions panel if you need to re-order the sequence in which they play.

1 To exclude a command from an action, click on the "run" checkmark (). The specific checkmark disappears from the column. Notice, also, the checkmark at the Action level turns red – this acts as an alert, so that even if the action is not expanded, you are aware that there is an excluded command in force. The red checkmark also appears at the Set level for the same purpose.

2 Click on the action name, then click the Play action button (▶) to run the action with the command excluded. To avoid confusion, and so that settings don't come back to haunt you, (unless you intend to run the action again with the same exclusion sometime soon), it is worth clicking the exclusion checkmark box again to reactivate the command.

To run an action and apply custom settings

There are often circumstances where you want to perform the same set of commands on multiple images, but you also want more granular control over each image.

Essentially, you want the consistency and speed of running a set of commands, but you also need to make individual judgments on certain settings for each image when you run the action.

You can do this by instructing the action to stop at any command that implements settings in a dialog box, and then display the dialog box so that you can make a manual intervention, creating the specific settings you want for that image, before continuing automatically with the subsequent steps in the action.

A modal command is one that requires you to press Enter or Return to apply its effect.

1 To pause an action to allow for individual custom settings, click in the "modal control" column for the command with the dialog box where you want to make these custom changes. Toggle on the dialog box (▣) to prompt the action to stop and display the dialog box so that you can make the custom settings. Notice also the Toggle active icon (▣) appears at the Action level – this acts as an alert, so that even if the action is not expanded, you are aware that there is a Toggle On/Off in force. The icon also appears at the Set level for the same purpose.

2 Click on the Action name, then click the Play action button (▶). The action runs all commands up to the Toggle On/Off command. It then displays the appropriate dialog box or panel so that you can create custom settings.

3 When you are satisfied with your changes, click OK in the dialog box, and the action continues to play.

In this example, a different Tint value was selected for the Black & White adjustment layer.

Insert a Stop

There may be times when you need to pause an action at a particular point so that you can perform a manual task that cannot be recorded as a step as part of the action. For example, you might be using an action for processing 20 product images in an identical way, with the exception that each image requires a specific caption added to it.

You can achieve this by adding a Stop.

The following walk-through, builds on the Polaroid example covered previously, but inserts a Stop to allow you add an individual caption to each image.

What "Stop" means in this instance is not stop, but "go ahead" – go ahead and stop the sequence of actions, so that you can perform the manual action required at this point in the sequence.

What "Continue" means is, don't stop to perform a manual action – continue without performing a manual task and allow the subsequent actions to play.

1 Open an image. In this example it's a 4 x 4 inches image at 300 ppi.

2 Recreate the steps described in the Polaroid setup in the previous example. This time, after the Move Current Layer command, select the Horizontal Type tool, then drag to define a text area in the space at the bottom of the image. Click the Commit button, or click the Type layer thumbnail to accept the type.

3 Go to the Actions panel menu (▦) and select Insert Stop. In the Record Stop dialog box, enter instructions to the user in the message box to explain the task they need to perform.

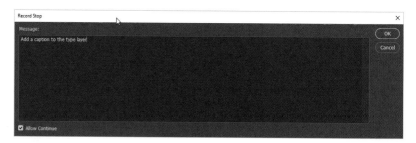

4 Switch on the Allow Continue checkbox – this includes a "Continue" button when the Message prompt appears

...cont'd

when you run the action. This gives the user the option of continuing with the commands in the action and not performing a manual task at the Stop.

Running an action with a Stop

1 When you run an action with a Stop, Photoshop proceeds to run all commands until it gets to the Stop. Then the Message prompt appears. If you selected the Allow

Continue checkbox, the Continue button is included in the Message prompt dialog. Click Continue if you don't want to perform the manual action. The prompt disappears, and Photoshop continues to run the remaining commands in the action.

2 Click the Stop button to pause the sequence of commands so that you can do something manually on the image. In this example, you could double-click the Type Layer thumbnail to activate the type layer. Enter text for the caption as required. Click the Commit button to accept changes to the type layer.

Wish you were here

3 Then, in the Actions panel, click the Play ( ) button again to resume playback of the remaining commands in the action.

The quickest way to format the type – apply a paragraph style. See pages 96-97 for information on setting up and applying paragraph styles.

Quick Export As

When you use the Quick Export As command, you are saving individual image assets out from the Photoshop document you are working on. This is not the same as using the Save As command. After a Quick Export As, you continue to work on the original document.

Web and app designers often find themselves working on projects where they need to generate a wide variety of image assets quickly, conveniently and with a minimum of fuss. The Quick Export As command goes a long way to satisfying this requirement – allowing you to quickly generate reusable image assets based on images, multiple layers, layer groups or Artboards.

The key to using Quick Export As – basically what makes it quick – are the predefined export preference settings that you set up. Essentially, you make your decision once, and then benefit from not having to make the same decisions every time you want to export image assets.

Exporting a (composite) image

1 In a multi-layered Photoshop document, with any single layer selected, choose File > Export > Quick Export As...

2 Depending on the export preferences set (see the colored panel opposite), if necessary, navigate to the folder where you want to save the composite image – the equivalent of a flattened file. Change the name if required. Click the Save button.

grad-blues-1336x
300_quickexport.
png

Quick Export Preferences

To change the file format from PNG, choose File > Export > Export Preferences to go directly to Export Preferences. Use the file format pop-up to select the file format you want to use.

The file format you select shows in the File > Quick Export As command after you OK the dialog box.

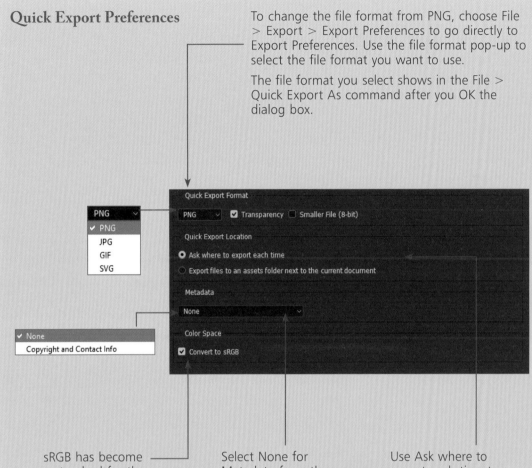

sRGB has become a standard for the display of images on screens and monitors. It is, arguably, not the best color space for images intended for print. sRGB is a color space developed by Microsoft and Hewlett -Packard for use with images intended for viewing on a screen.

Select None for Metadata from the pop-up to strip out any metadata saved with the image. Select Copyright and Contact Info if you want to retain basic metadata saved with the image.

Use Ask where to export each time to display the standard Save dialog box to specify where you want to save the exported image assets.

If you select Export files to an assets folder, Photoshop creates a folder that it names using the image's filename with "...assets" appended, and saves files to this location alongside the original file.

...cont'd

Creating layer-based image assets

1 Select the layer or layers in the Layers panel. Multiple layers can be consecutive or non-consecutive.

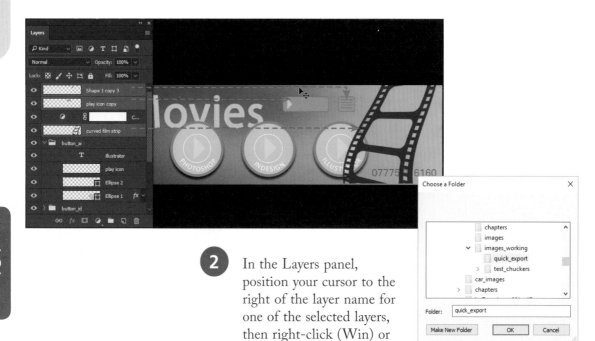

2 In the Layers panel, position your cursor to the right of the layer name for one of the selected layers, then right-click (Win) or ctrl + click (Mac).

3 Select Quick Export as PNG. Navigate to the folder where you want to save the file. Either accept the default name – to use the name of the layer – or enter a new name. Click Save.

4 The result is a flattened image(s) in PNG file format, which includes transparency (provided that you haven't changed export settings).

curved film strip.png

grad-blues-1336x 300_quickexport. psd

play icon copy.png

Shape 1 copy 3.png

To export a layer group

A powerful technique is to group together related elements in a composition in a layer group: you can then export the layer group as a single image asset.

button_psd.png

1 Select the layer group in the Layers panel. Position your cursor to the right of the layer group name, then right-click/ctrl + click.

2 Select Quick Export As PNG.

3 Navigate to the folder where you want to save the file. Either accept the default name – replicates the name of the layer group – or enter a new name. Click Save.

4 What you get is a flattened image in PNG file format that includes transparency – provided that you haven't changed export settings.

To export Artboard documents

The Quick Export As command is also available when you are working in an Artboard document.

1 It doesn't matter whether you have an Artboard or a layer within an Artboard selected.

2 Select Quick Export As PNG. Navigate to folder. In a multi-Artboard file, each Artboard is exported as a composite image file.

Artboard 1.png   Artboard 2.png   Artboard 3.png

185

Export As

Export As is the new powerhouse for exporting images, multiple layers, layer groups and Artboards. Where Quick Export As is fast, convenient and unfussy, the Export As command delivers a more precise and granular set of controls and options.

Generate multiple image sizes

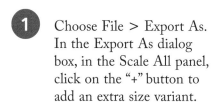

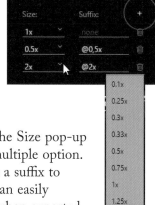

You can change the suffix from the default size indicator (@0,5x etc.) if required.

1 Choose File > Export As. In the Export As dialog box, in the Scale All panel, click on the "+" button to add an extra size variant.

2 In the Size column, click on the Size pop-up button (▼) to select a size multiple option. Photoshop automatically adds a suffix to each size variant so that you can easily distinguish the files by name when exported.

3 Create settings in the Settings section on the right-hand side of the Export As dialog box.

Click the Trash button for a size variant to remove it from the export list.

4 Click Export All to create image assets and remain working in the original Photoshop document.

> bk_ies_PSD_tipstricks_02nov › images_working › medieval_project_assets

medieval2.jpg   medieval2@0,5x.j   medieval2@0,25x
                  pg   .jpg

Exporting multiple layers

1 In the Layers panel, select multiple layers – these can be consecutive or non-consecutive.

2 Choose File > Export > Export As. Each layer appears as an individual entry on the left. Specify size variants you want to create (see above).

(continued on page 188)

...cont'd

Export As

Use the Scale All pane to specify multiple size variants to export. Image assets are exported using the settings available in the File Settings pane on the right.

Choose a file format from the Format pop-up menu. The settings available change, depending on the format you choose.

Use the Image Size controls if you want to adjust the size of the original image before exporting. Either enter new pixel dimensions or enter a Scale amount.

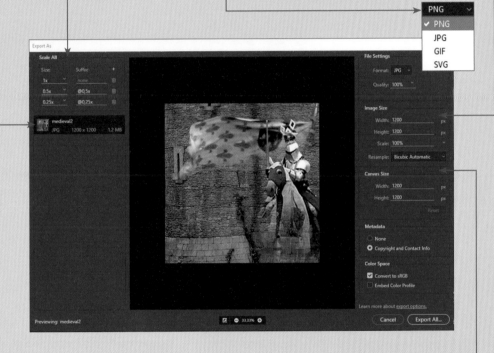

The optimization thumbnail readout updates according to the format and settings you choose:

Default Canvas Size dimensions are the same as the image size. Increase the Canvas Size settings to add a border or padding around the exported image assets.

...cont'd

3 If required, select a specific image in the Scale All pane, then create export settings in the right-hand File Settings pane for each layer individually, or multiple-select layers to apply the same settings. The option to create settings for individual assets can be useful when some images, for example, optimize better as GIF than JPEG.

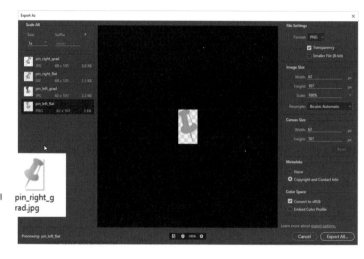

pin_left_flat
.png   pin_left_gra
d.jpg   pin_right_fl
at.gif   pin_right_g
rad.jpg

Exporting Artboards

1 When using Export As for an Artboard document, it doesn't matter whether you have an Artboard or a layer within an Artboard selected.

2 Select File > Export As. Create the settings you require, then click the Export All button.

Index